HAUNTED EVERETT, WASHINGTON

DEBORAH CUYLE

Haunted America

Published by Haunted America
A Division of The History Press
Charleston, SC
www.historypress.com

Cover image courtesy of author.

First published 2019

Manufactured in the United States

ISBN 9781467142847

Library of Congress Control Number: 2019943359

DEDICATION

Some things have to be believed to be seen.
—Ralph Hodgson

Death is no more than passing from one room into another.
—Helen Keller

It would be a shame to dedicate this book to anyone other than David Dilgard of the Everett Public Library. His unwavering devotion to the history of Everett was incredible. Unfortunately, David is no longer with us, but I hope his spirit is still roaming the Northwest Room at the library he so loved. He will be remembered for his storytelling, fascinating tours, historical books and preservation efforts. The manuscripts and files he left have been a great and valuable resource for many of these ghost stories. He had a liking for anything haunted, and he would always chuckle and say, "None of us gets out of here alive!" Perhaps David now roams the halls of the library with the spirit of Alice McFarland Duryee (1875–1914) who served as the first head librarian at the Everett Public Library in 1898. Originally from Maine, Alice was an early Everett pioneer who also had a great love and devotion for the town's library.

This book is also dedicated to all of my friends, my son Dane and every other fellow ghost hunter out there. Without them, I would be wandering around dark rooms all by myself with my EMF detector and ghost radar, which wouldn't be very much fun at all.

Happy ghost hunting!

—Deborah Cuyle

These two images depict early Everett. The top image is of Hewitt and Wetmore Avenues with horse-drawn carriages and trolley cars. The bottom is of Hewitt Avenue with fancy new automobiles. *Everett Public Library.*

CONTENTS

PREFACE

If you knew that your life was merely a phase or short, short segment of your entire existence, how would you live? Knowing nothing "real" was at risk, what would you do? You'd live a gigantic, bold, fun, dazzling life. You know you would. That's what the ghosts want us to do—all the exciting things they no longer can do.
—Chuck Palahniuk

This book project was inspired by the ghost stories of my friends who live in Everett. Some of them told me that they felt an eerie hand touch the back of their neck while at the old Everett Theatre. Others claimed that they saw apparitions while wandering the grounds of Evergreen Cemetery. Paranormal researchers from the area shared photographs, EVPs and personal experiences from their investigations with me. I love all of the lore, legends and ghost stories from Everett that I have been told throughout the years, so I gathered them all to share in this book in the hopes that it brings Everett, the old mill town, back to life with its fascinating and frightening tales.

My interest and respect for the early pioneers, my fascination with Washington's local history and my personal passion for old buildings also inspired me to write this book. It was fun to walk the same streets as those early pioneers and think of how it was for them back in the old days. History is full of people who haunt us, who want to be recognized and never forgotten for what they did, what they created, what they offered. This book is about those fascinating spirits—the spirited people who made Everett what it is today.

Top: Street lights and automobiles adorn Hewitt and Rucker Avenues. *Bottom*: This 1900 postcard by photographer Norman Edson shows Hewitt Avenue looking west with the Mohawk Block, Mitchell Hotel (later known as the Cascadian Apartments), Grand Leader Department Store and Lobby Saloon. *Everett Public Library.*

The stories in this book are all told for fun and for the love of history and lore. This book is not intended to be a nonfiction project, despite the hundreds of hours I spent hunched over, reading and researching. While writing this book, I found conflicting dates and inconsistent historic details, so please take these stories for what they are. I tried to be as accurate with names, dates and details as I possibly could, but this, ultimately, is just a fun book full of tales of mischievous ghosts and history of the town.

Ghost stories, legends and folklore exist in every town, big and small, new and old. Human beings are fascinated with the afterlife and are eager to somehow capture proof of the spirit world. But what are these spirits that people are so eager to find proof of? Hauntings that are created by accidents or incidences of trauma are called "residual hauntings" and are the most common form. Ghosts in residual hauntings tend hang around because they have become trapped by past traumatic events. A kind nudge to "go to the other side" is sometimes all it takes to get the spirit to move on. Another type of haunting is called "intelligent," in which the ghosts can communicate and interact with the living, which cause the more classic types of paranormal activity. When spirits use their energy to move objects, make noises or make items disappear and reappear, it is known as a "poltergeist haunting." This type of activity is what I have found to be fairly common, and it is typically just playful.

Apparitions and odors are the most common forms of paranormal activity, although odors are impossible to "capture" and prove. Strange noises are also common forms of paranormal activity. These noises often imitate the sounds of human, environmental and animal activities such as crying and moaning, but they can also imitate the sounds of chairs moving or dishes breaking. Paranormal activity can also come in the form of a crisis apparition, or the appearance of a passed loved one offering comfort. These are single events that typically occur when a living person undergoes a personal crisis. Unfortunately, these crisis apparitions are commonly shrugged off as daydreams or ignored and labeled as strange events caused by personal stress. However, I would like for my readers to keep in mind how much energy it takes for a spirit to manifest itself. It is an extremely hard task, so it is very important that the spirit is acknowledged and given words of thanks. While single instances of paranormal activity are exciting, the apparition of an animal or a person is only considered to be a haunting when it continues to appear in the same location.

I have personally experienced so many unexplainable things that I can no longer doubt the existence of ghosts and spirits. I have had my cheek pinched by an unseen hand after catching a faint whiff of Johnson's baby powder. I have had my arm grabbed and twisted by the spirit of an angry man after researching a local building. I have heard creepy conversations through my cellphone along with the sounds of both an old rotary dial phone and a push button (both of which no longer existed in my home). My most frightening experience happened while I was in the basement of an old jail. I saw the dark apparition of a man out of the corner of my eye and heard the sound of him pounding against the stone wall, demanding to leave the prison.

Not all paranormal experiences are scary. I have had others that were very comforting and welcome in my life. I sometimes catch the smell of my departed mother's perfume, Jovan Musk, in my times of need. It's her way of letting me know she is still watching over me, and it is my favorite ghostly activity. I also once found a scratchy, handwritten note from my deceased grandfather while I was living in upstate New York that read, "MOW THE YARD!" He was obviously extremely irritated that I had left my lawn un-mowed, and upon investigation, I found that the grass had indeed grown up to my knees! How did my grandfather *know* his lawn was being neglected from beyond the grave?

Don't dismiss those signs and hard-to-forget dreams in which your loved ones either give you clues, offer advice or simply let you know they still watch over you—they are all signs of the afterlife.

I believe in ghosts. I believe in haunted places. I believe that there is more to our lives than just this realm.

ACKNOWLEDGEMENTS

Behind every man now alive stand thirty ghosts,
for that is the ratio by which the dead outnumber the living.
—Arthur C. Clarke, 2001: A Space Odyssey

There are many people I would like to thank for coming with me on this endeavor and for their help and guidance, without whom this book would not have been possible. My wonderful editor, Laurie Krill, has been such a pleasure to work with along with all the other incredible people at Arcadia Publishing and The History Press. Their mission to promote local history is passionate and infectious, and I am blessed to work on my books with them.

Lisa Labovitch at the Everett Public Library has been a constant source of help and inspiration.

Jeffrey Pearce and Jeanne Leader, along with several others from Everett Community College, were so generous in allowing me to hear their ghost stories.

Raven Corvus from White Noise Paranormal in the greater Seattle area was a great resource for paranormal stories and excellent photographs. Of course, I would also like to mention Judi Ramsey from Artisans Mercantile in Snohomish, who has been very supportive throughout the years. I would also like to thank my fellow book lover and ghost enthusiast, Sheryl Palmer, who always spends time with me at signings, keeping me amused.

My appreciation is extended to all those who took the time to share with me their personal ghost stories and experiences. Without them, this book would not have had the extra flair that I love so much.

As always, I want to thank every single person who does what they can to preserve history—whether you volunteer at your local historical society, maintain old cemeteries and gravestones or simply research private genealogies, I thank you. In this fast-paced and high-tech world, the past can, unfortunately, be easily forgotten. Every effort made to maintain and record valuable data, photographs, diaries, documents and records is of the upmost importance for future generations.

I only have one request: Please do not enter any of the locations listed throughout this book without the expressed permission of the property or business owners. Some of these locations have, unfortunately, experienced property destruction in the past due to trespassing, and their owners would like to avoid future damage. Thank you for your understanding.

Introduction

The people do not realize the magnitude of this undertaking or appreciate the extent of the forces that will build a great city here…already we have spent $5,000,000 in preliminary work in Everett.
—interview with Charles Colby, 1893

The first permanent settler to the area (aside from the several Native American tribes that already lived there) we now call Port Gardner was a man from Massachusetts named Dennis Brigham, who arrived around 1861. The farmer claimed 160 acres and built a small cabin.

In the 1890s, the muddy streets of Everett were lined with small cedar shacks and grubby tents—all nestled along the beautiful waterfront, where many men were eager to build a new city and, hopefully, prosper. The City of Smokestacks was built on the products produced from the many pulp, paper, shingle and lumber mills in the area that were filled with hardworking men. The overgrown timber in the region was a big draw to many, as it was worth millions in profit. Others had their eyes set on mining the area for its coal and various precious metals. The Pacific Northwest seemed rich in possibility; the soil was fertile, the water was plentiful and men came from as far as New York to seize their share. It is rumored that if there were no hotel rooms available, some eager businessmen would sleep in their handmade coffins, which they would sell later for a nice profit.

Unidentified people on Chestnut Street and Hewitt Avenue on January 14, 1892. This picture shows signs for Robinson-Moore Real Estate and the People's Market is in view. *Everett Public Library, photographer Frank La Roche.*

At this time, it was rumored that the great James Hill, the railroad tycoon and empire builder, was planning to bring his Great Northern Railroad line through the Cascade Mountains, all the way to the bay of Port Gardner. This stirred a lot of confidence in American investors. Henry Hewitt Jr. played a large role in the initial development of Everett. He was a successful lumber magnate and investor, and in 1890, he formed the Everett Land Company, which was located on the corner of Pacific and Oakes Streets, with the help of Charles Colby, a New York banker, and John Rockefeller. If the famous J.D. Rockefeller himself was interested in the mining and industrial aspects in the town, then building the area up must have been a good idea.

Soon, more powerful men became involved. Colgate Hoyt and Charles Wetmore were interested in the new town, and James Hill, still interested in bringing his railroad through, got Frederick Weyerhauser interested in the upcoming area through the lure of its heavy timber resources. With the meeting of all these great minds and money, Everett was bound to be

John Rockefeller (1839–1937) was one of the wealthiest men in American history. Born in upstate New York to a con artist, he began working hard in his early teens. His personal goal was to live to be one hundred years old, but he missed it by two years. *Washington State Historical Society.*

successful. Even the town's name was decided upon while the men all dined at Colby's home in 1890. Hewitt remarked that Colby's fifteen-year-old son, Everett, had an incredibly energetic personality and suggested that he fit the ideal image of the town. They all agreed and named the town Everett. In 1892, the census recorded a population of 4,500 in Everett. Men in Everett had cleared six hundred acres, costing the town $50,000, and another $250,000 had to be spent on twelve miles of street grading, eight miles of which were planked, and thirteen miles of sidewalks. Mud control was of the utmost importance in a town where it rained so much.

The city was certainly bustling by 1901, and the *Oregon, Washington and Alaska Gazetteer* from that year certainly summed it up well when it stated:

> *In 1901, the government has appropriated $422,000 to improve the harbor in Everett. The dense forests of pine, fir and cedar create the need for nine saw mills that can produce one million feet per day, ten shingle mills that cut two million shingles per day, three large ship yards and Sumner Iron Works. The Everett Pulp and Paper Mill just south of the city is one of the largest in the U.S. and employees two hundred men turning out twenty tons of paper daily. The Everett Smelting and*

Refining Company sit on twenty-five acres and produces two hundred tons per day. Everett has four large, brick schools including a school of music and oratory. It has a new hospital, seven hundred new homes, ten miles of paving, fifty new business buildings and four thousand more residents in just one year!

Everett grew into quite a large town, and it is even greater today. The city, now the seventh largest in Washington, is home to over 100,000 people and growing rapidly. The town's semi-complicated and fascinating history is full of stories about local taverns and banks, mills and shipyards, land claims and land losses…all brought about by both the rich and the poor.

One of the city's greatest assets is the deep waters of the bay. In the late nineteenth century, huge logs could float easily down the rivers to later be cut into timber and loaded onto ships, where they were exported to other countries, eager to purchase the valuable timber. At a banquet in February 1892 at the Bay View Hotel, the railroad tycoon James Hill said this of Everett, "All we ask is for you to have the stuff to ship! The distance from here to Chicago is between 230 and 250 miles less than from San Francisco to Chicago.…Your timber interests are your greatest resource of wealth!" The crowd cheered at this assertion, and Hill was right; Puget Sound Shingles brought in $25,000 cash per day.

Everett had four shingle mills that were cranking out almost 500,000 shingles per day. Port Gardner Red Cedar Lumber Company, located at the end of the Fourteenth Street wharf, employed forty-four men and cut 250,000 shingles per day, Blackman Brothers had twenty men and cut 100,000 shingles per day, the Everett Shingle Company had twenty men as well and cut another 90,000 per day and Darling & Allen on the bay side cut 50,000 per day and also employed twenty men. If these figures are accurate, each man would have been responsible for over 4,000 shingles per day.

It is no wonder as to why the men wanted better working conditions for this extremely dangerous and labor-intensive job. Many of these men suffered and sometimes died from "cedar asthma," which was caused by fine sawdust getting into their lungs. Do any of these men still linger around their old mills? Do any of their wives hang around in spirit form?

The spirits of pioneers from Everett's past want to be remembered and they their stories told to anyone who will listen. These ghosts are a part of Everett's fascinating history, and many have continued to haunt their buildings by the waterfront for over a century. Many locals say they feel

The Everett Land Company, in 1893, listed Henry Hewitt Jr. as president, Gardner Colby as treasurer, E.B. Bartlett as vice president, Henry Schenck as secretary and Schuyler Duryee as general manager. Henry Hewitt Jr. (1840–1918) was born in England. He then relocated to Washington in 1888 when he heard of the valuable land available in the Pacific Northwest. *Everett Public Library.*

Colgate (1849–1922) and Lida Hoyt sit elegantly together on a boat. Colgate was an early investor in Everett and one of its founding fathers. He was also the director of the Oregon Railway and Navigation Company and a New York banker. *Wikipedia.*

the spirits of the early Everett forerunners still roaming the town's streets and buildings. Perhaps they are curious about all the changes the town has experienced. Can you imagine a ghost from the late 1800s looking around at the buildings and technology we use today? They would be frightened, amused, intrigued and probably very jealous. As long as locals and tourists remain open-minded about Everett's ghostly past, there will be plenty of haunts around the town to enjoy.

With the timber boom, early Everett was littered with large tree stumps and deep, thick mud. Here, the railroad right-of-way sign is pictured between the towns of Everett and nearby Lowell on January 14, 1892. *Everett Public Library, photographer Frank La Roche.*

A story from Randy in Snohomish:

> *I was walking to my favorite breakfast spot in Everett when I walked past this bench* [and] *heard a female voice very distinctly say, ":No one ever notices me!" Startled, I turned back around to see who* [had] *said it, but no one was there. It was* [a] *very clear voice and rather loud. Another time, at the same spot, I thought I saw a partial silhouette of a woman wearing a white blouse or sweater sitting* [on the bench]. *A third time, I was walking past, and I heard what sounded like a woman running in high heels. Again, no one was there.*

1
HISTORIC EVERETT THEATRE

There are an infinite number of universes existing side by side and through which our consciousness's constantly pass. In these universes, all possibilities exist. You are alive in some, long dead in others, and never existed in still others. Many of our "ghosts" could indeed be visions of people going about their business in a parallel universe or another time or both.
—*Paul F. Eno,* Faces at the Window

One of the most well-known haunts in town is the Everett Theatre on Colby Avenue.

The glamorous and exciting lives actors and actresses enjoy is a hard one to leave behind once dead, and this is no exception for theater's ghostly performers. The century old Historic Everett Theatre is well known for its phantoms and regular apparitions. Many people have experienced what they feel is hard evidence that the theater is truly haunted.

James Hill, the Great Northern Railroad tycoon, backed a project to build the theater with money from his Everett Improvement Company, and the theater opened in 1901. On a tragic winter's night in 1923, the building experienced a fire. For a long three hours, flames continued to destroy the building. It started in the orchestra pit and caused fatal damage. Plans to quickly rebuild the theater started almost immediately.

The eerie, yet alluring, century-old theater located at 2911 Colby Avenue is known for its hauntings and ghostly apparitions. Local ghost hunting events, tours and paranormal investigations are scheduled regularly. Almost

The historic Everett Theatre on Colby is the most well known and active haunt in Everett. For over one hundred years, the theater has been entertaining locals and travelers. Many ghost hunting expeditions occur in the building, and most investigators do not go away disappointed! *White Noise Paranormal Society and The Historic Everett Theatre.*

After a number of alterations to the 1924 façade, the Everett Theatre has been restored to resemble its beautiful appearance displayed in this 1929 photograph. *Everett Public Library, Juleen, J. A. Collection #J1796.*

everyone who has visited the building has experienced something— an unexplained movement out of the corner of their eye, the slight touch of a web-like substance on their face or even the evidence of ghostly voices. The spirits have become so well known in the community that the theater started to hold ghost hunting events. The theater even attracted the attention of KING-TV and *Evening Magazine*.

In a recent video I watched from the theater, a curtain can be seen moving with a chandelier or light swinging back and forth behind it. Shapes of light also fly through the air on the video, then disappear. When people physically researched the area, they could not find a light anywhere aside from the exit sign over the door. What are the lights that were caught on camera? How can light appear on a video that is not caught by the human eye? Owners, employees and patrons of the theater all have the same questions when it comes to their experiences there.

Locals and employees of the theater believe that the spirit of Al Jolson, an actor who performed on the Everett Theatre stage from 1906 to 1915,

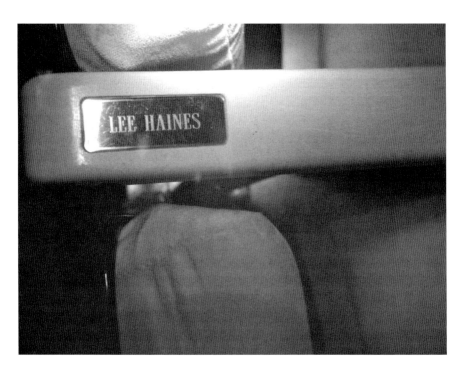

Ghost hunters gathered evidence of an actual spirit sitting in the seat of former theater employee Lee Hines. Many believe Hines's ghost still roams the building. *White Noise Paranormal and Everett Public Library.*

haunts the theater. He had an incredible and unforgettable smile when he was alive, and it what later earned his spirit the nickname of Smilin' Al. He was also an active advocate for civil rights on the stage, and he fought for the right of African Americans to perform in a time when that was not common.

Many also believe that the ghost of a former theater employee is still roaming the building. Lee Hines worked in the production room for sixteen years, and he loved the place so much that the theater named his old seat after him. Ghost hunters believe they were able to gather evidence of an actual spirit sitting in Lee Hines's seat. The team was able to record a heat spike of 77.1 degrees in the old theater seat when the room itself was very cold.

When did the ghostly hauntings at the old Everett Theatre actually begin? Legend says that the spirits were not stirred until 1993, when the theater underwent some serious renovations. It is suggested that renovations and remodels frequently prompt hauntings, because the construction aggravates and frustrates ghosts. Since the building had been vacant for years prior to the remodel, it is no wonder the ghosts did not want all the noise and disturbance. Smilin'Al and his long-deceased friends quickly began slamming doors, moving items, touching workers and carrying out other mischievous activity as if to say, "Go away! We liked having the place all to ourselves!"

The following are a number of ghost stories from owners, employees and volunteers of the Historic Everett Theatre:

A collection of stories from Iris and Laura, employees of the theater:

> [At the theater,] *we were doing both the male & female versions of* The Odd Couple. *At the time, our sound & light boards were up on the balcony. During the women's performance, Curt Shriner* [the owner of the theater] *would* [run] *the lights and sound cues, and during the male performance, Iris Lilly would* [run] *lights and sound. Iris was up doing sound and lights, and she missed a couple cues, because someone had sat down right next to her and was touching her arm. The following night, during the* [women's] *performance, Curt went up to work the lights and sound. As he sat down, he said, "Okay you, don't bother me. I'm working here." There was nobody up there except him, but, suddenly, he was hit on the back of his head with a*

crumpled-up [piece of] *paper. He immediately looked* [around], *but there was nobody there.*

During a ghost hunt [for my friend Laura Shriner's birthday], *Iris Lilly and Curt Shriner were down in the greenroom. Iris saw movement in the mirror and turned her head to look....* [She] *saw a woman in a floor-length, white dress come* [through] *a door that was locked* [with a latch and key lock]. *She turned and ran up the back stairs toward the stage.*

We had a band performing [at the theater] *one night when a woman came up to a couple of* [our] *volunteers and asked if someone could ask the woman in the long black dress to stop looking through the curtain because it* [was] *very disruptive. Iris Lilly went back stage* [to look for the woman, but] *there were no women. She asked the performers that were down in the greenroom and back stage if* [they had seen] *a woman in a black dress. They said there were no women at all. As I went back out, a man sitting in the audience said, "Thank you, that woman was very disruptive." So, two separate people saw a woman that wasn't there.*

In 2015, Curt and Craig Shriner [the owners of the theater] *were in the projecting room* [where the sound and light boards are now] *and were talking about construction plans for the room. Suddenly, a garbage can* [was] *lifted off the floor...dropped...and circled its rim* [before it] *stopped. Craig said, "Did you see that?" Curt replied, "Yeah, stuff like that happens here all the time."*

During the production of Varney the Vampire, *Laura Shriner had to wear a mask. She always put her mask in the same place.* [Once,] *she went to get her mask and it was missing. She asked everyone if they saw her mask. Nobody saw it or knew where it was. Everyone looked everywhere,* [but] *they couldn't find it. Luckily, she had a second mask and went* [to get] *it. On the day of the last* [performance], *Laura was heading toward the stage to go down to the greenroom when she saw the mask hanging on part of the stage. Several people had looked there,* [but it hadn't been] *there. Laura asked the janitor, and he said he had not seen it before that day either.*

We were doing a public ghost hunt [at the theater]. *There was* [one] *group in the greenroom, one on the balcony and one in the front basement.*

Each group had two recorders. Someone from each group said they asked,
"If there is anyone here, could they tell us their name." Some people heard
a female voice say a first and last name (unfortunately, I can't remember
the name), but not everyone heard [it]. *When we all gathered together in*
the main house, we discovered that the voice was captured on some of the
recorders but not all of them. At least one recorder from each area picked up
the voice. In a couple of the cases, [the] *recorders were right next to each*
other, [but] *only one picked it up.*

The night before our first public ghost hunt, Laura Shriner, Iris Lilly, Chris
Osburn and Veronica Calhoun (employees of the theater) decided to do a
private hunt to try out our equipment. On the EVP, we kept hearing a name:
Red, Ned or Ed, [but] *we couldn't quite make it out. We also kept hearing*
the same voice saying, "Ladder." We really had no idea what that meant,
and at the time, we didn't know of any connection between the two. The
following weekend, we were having a concert [at the theater]. *A woman*
came up to Laura Shriner and said that [her friend's father, who] *used*
to work at the theater, had just died. She said her friend had something that
her dad wanted to give back to the theater. Laura [told the woman to*
have her friend] *call her. When she called,* [the woman's friend] *told*
Laura that her [dad worked] *at the theater years ago…in the boiler room*
and the projection room.… [She said] *that he had really loved it and had*
become upset when the previous owners had turned [the theater] *into a*
triplex cinema.…She said before her dad died, he [had] *told her he wanted*
to make sure that the ladders he had were returned to the theater. They were
the ladders originally used when putting up signs etc. Laura said that was
nice of him and asked [the woman for] *her dad's name was so* [the*
theater] *could honor him by naming a room after him.* [The woman]
said, "Ed McMurray." It then dawned on us [that] *the name we* [had]
picked up was Ed and he was trying to tell us about the ladders.

We put electronic recorders around the theater and carry one with us when
we do ghost hunts. I have hundreds of EVPs. Some are category A, which
are very clear, and some are not as clear. Some of the clearer EVPs include:
a little child saying, "Mommy;" names of ghosts that are always there
(Brittany, Bridgit, Mike, Ed, Steven, Al); a female voice saying "Daschle,
if you don't want that, I will take it;" [voices] *saying our names: Veronica,*
Laura, Chris, Iris, Donald; our dad, who died in 2016, said his name,
Coda, and told us, "Go have some pie for you sweetheart." [He] *had a very*
distinct sneeze, and we recorded his sneeze.

The original theater, built in 1898, was a sight to behold as shown in this 1902 Kirk and Seely photogravure booklet. The theater opened on November 4, 1901, and is said to be haunted by Smilin' Al, a former entertainer. *Everett Public Library.*

Another time, Curtis was giving a tour, talking about the fires that happened [at the theater]. *When he mentioned the fire in the 1920s, a female's voice came through the recorder that said, "That's how I died."*

A ghost story from Izzy, a volunteer at the theater:

Earlier this year, during a concert, Iris Lilly was showing a couple of men the ghost pictures on her phone. One of the guys was excited about it and said it would be cool if the ghost gave them a show that night. The other guy said he didn't believe in [ghosts, because] *he had never seen anything to make him think* [they] *could be* [real]. *At the end of the concert, the two men were looking at the pictures on the walls. They went to the corner near the volunteer closet. Izzy, one of our volunteers, went to the closet and put her name tag and light away. She made sure she locked the door and then double checked that it was closed. She started to leave, and got about half way through the lobby, when the guy who did not believe in ghosts ran after her and grabbed her shoulder. He was almost hyperventilating and loudly said, "You closed and locked the door, right?" Izzy told him she did.*

He was very animated, and [he] *pointed to the corner and asked* [her] *why it* [had opened] *on its own. Izzy went to check, and the door was open. The other guy told her that the door* [had] *just opened by itself. The guy who didn't believe before, left saying he* [believed].

A ghost story from Rich, a volunteer at the theater:

The following week, another volunteer, Rich, came up to me and told me he tried to close the door, but it felt like someone was pushing [it] *open. He said he opened it and checked to see if anything was in the way, but there was nothing in the way. He tried again, and it still felt like someone was pushing the door. On his third try, the door closed. He was adamant that nothing was in the way and that he checked the door jams and all around the door.*

A ghost story from Randy Randall:

Years ago, our sound board was on the balcony, off to the side. Laura Shriner was up there doing the sound cues. Another guy was doing the lights.

The fascinating world of the theater has always intrigued people, and the seldom seen backstage area is where the ghosts hang out! An eerie face was captured on camera when no one was there. Ghost hunters pledge they saw many other strange happenings while touring the old theater. *White Noise Paranormal Society.*

THE HISTORIC EVERETT THEATR

Helen Keller   Fatty Arbuckle   Nat King Cole   Cecil B. DeMille   Helen Hayes   Lillian Russell   Ruth St

Laura was waiting for her cue when the guy kept whispering, "Laura, look." She looked over, and he was pointing to the empty cassette case. The case was rotating like someone had their finger on the middle of the case [while] *flicking the side of the case, making it turn in circles. Neither he nor Laura had touched the case.*

A ghost story from a paranormal investigator, Raven Corvus of White Noise Paranormal:

We had a few really freaky things happen [during our investigation]. *We heard a woman's voice all night, and* [we] *even got an EVP of a scream. We were able to hear it when we did an EVP session downstairs!*

A ghost story from June Antoinette Nixon:

About seven years ago, [when] *I was in another group…we investigated the old Everett Theater. There wasn't a lot of activity going on at first, so most of the investigators left around 2:30 in the morning,* [leaving only] *my friend Jay and me. We did get* [some] *interesting* [evidence] *and an EVP* [when] *we asked if the spirits* [if] *knew the names of anyone*

ISHED 1901

Could the ghosts be one of these wonderful performers who once graced the stage in Everett? (*Left to right*) Helen Keller, Fatty Arbuckle, Nat King Cole, Cecil B. DeMille, Helen Hayes, Lillian Russell, Ruth St. Denis, John Barrymore, George Cohen, Al Jolson, John Phillip Sousa, Lon Chaney and Mack Swain. *The Historic Everett Theatre.*

George Cohen   Al Jolson   John Phillip Sousa   Lon Chaney   Mack Swain

who worked there….We got the name Joe pretty loud, [which] *happened to be the* [name of the] *night watchman at the time. We were packing up all of the equipment about four o'clock in the morning; I was in the Green Room down in the lower level and kept hearing Jay stomping and walking above me. I was wondering what he was doing,* [so I looked] *up the stairs and* [saw] *him standing at the top, in the shadows,* [before walking] *back up. I called him on the walkie-talkie, asked him what he was doing and* [told him] *to stop making so much racket. He responded back to me by saying that he thought* [I was the one] *making a lot of racket downstairs and that he was on the top floor taking apart the tripods and cameras. I paused and said, "You mean you haven't been down here? But I saw someone standing at the top of the steps before they went down to the greenroom!" I assumed someone* [else] *must* [have been] *inside* [the building]. *We both scoured every inch of the theater, checked all the doors to make sure they were locked, checked the bathrooms, the closets. No one was there at four o'clock in the morning. It was only us.*

Then, we heard the old elevator start up, which doesn't move unless someone pushes the button. After that, we heard someone run up or down the steps where Jay [had been] *putting up the equipment. There was absolutely no one in the building except for us. There weren't any shops open or people anywhere to be seen on the streets at that time of morning. So, we sat on the stage for another hour, just listening. We kept hearing the footsteps all around us.* [We] *heard the elevator, which was very loud at the time, going up and down. Then, both of us heard a woman, very loudly, from backstage say, "HEY!"* Then [all the noises] *disappeared around 5:30 in the morning.*

A ghost story from Connie from Everett:

I love to visit the Everett Theatre for various shows....More than once, I [have sworn that I saw] *ghosts and orbs out of the corners of my eye.*

Aside from all of the theater's resident spirits, many famous performers have enjoyed working on the stage at the historic Everett Theatre, including the legendary pianist and vocalist Nat King Cole. The theater has entertained the citizens of Everett for over one hundred years, and it will continue to do so long into the future.

OTHER NEARBY HAUNTED THEATERS

Many nearby towns have also experienced ghosts in their theaters. Seattle has several haunted theaters, as well as Kent and Edmonds. The Edmonds Theater on Main Street is said to have a male ghost that is seen as a glowing aura. In Seattle, ghosts have been seen in the Moore Theatre, the Harvard Exit Theatre, the Egyptian Theatre and the Neptune Theatre.

2
RUCKER MANSION

I don't believe that ghosts are "spirits of the dead" because I don't believe in death.
In the multiverse, once you're possible, you exist. And once you exist, you exist forever
one way or another. Besides, death is the absence of life, and the ghosts I've met are
very much alive. What we call ghosts are lifeforms just as you and I are.
—*Paul F. Eno,* Footsteps in the Attic

One of Everett's most notorious haunts is the Rucker Mansion on Laurel Drive. The fabulous, 7,800-square-foot Rucker Mansion was built in 1905 by an unknown architect. It is currently a private residence listed on the National Historic Register. When Bethel Rucker, one of Jane Rucker's sons, became engaged, he quickly purchased the most beautiful three-acre home site he could find on the water in Everett. He built the luxurious home for $40,000 as a wedding surprise for his new bride, Ruby Brown, who came from the Dakotas to marry Bethel the previous year. The unknown architect combined several styles of architecture in the structure of the home, including Italian, Queen Anne and Georgian Revival. The home has a breathtaking view of the harbor from many of its windows, a magnificent ballroom on the third floor and a card and billiards room in the basement.

The Rucker brothers filed for a fifty-acre plat in 1890 in a town that they hoped to call Port Gardner. The family's investments in real estate, banking and timber during Everett's boomtown years proved to be quite profitable for the whole family. The brothers also ran a successful sawmill in the Lake Stevens area and the Big Four Inn near Darrington.

Above: The Rucker Mansion is located on Laurel Drive and was built by the Rucker brothers. The Rucker family settled in Everett prior to the Rockefeller boom. The mansion still has a sweeping view of the water and is listed in the National Register of Historic Places. *Deborah Cuyle.*

Right: Jane Morris Rucker (1830–1907) was the mother of Wyatt (1857–1931) and Bethel (1862–1945). For unknown reasons, she died by suicide after jumping out of a window in her Everett mansion. *Everett Public Library.*

The Rucker brothers, Wyatt and Bethel (*right*), came from Tacoma in 1890 and bought land in the Port Gardner peninsula area. The brothers' investments were of utmost importance to Everett's early development, and they later owned a huge lumber mill in Lake Stevens and the Big Four Inn near Darrington. *Deborah Cuyle.*

It is said that early on, the ever-smart Wyatt Rucker bought a rowboat and promptly began "fishing for salmon" on the bay. His *real* interest, though, was in determining how deep the waters were in various parts of the bay, because they envisioned creating a port at the area near the mouth of the Snohomish River to attract the attention of James Hill and the Great Northern Railway. After these "fishing trips," Wyatt was inspired to purchase a 160-acre waterfront farm there—a steal at just $35,000. A few months later, the brothers bought another eight hundred acres, and on August 22, 1890, the brothers petitioned to name the area Port Gardner. The men started the Rucker Bank, which was located at 1602 Hewitt Avenue in Everett, with Wyatt Rucker as its president and Bethel Rucker as its cashier. Wyatt also developed the Everett Improvement Company with J.T. McChesney as president and Edward Mony as secretary and Wyatt as treasurer, and it was located at 1713 Hewitt Avenue.

Amid all the family's good fortune, and for reasons unknown, the elderly Jane Rucker leapt to her death from a bedroom window in 1907 and died at the age of seventy-seven. The Rucker Mausoleum, located in Everett's Evergreen Cemetery, was built in her honor by her loving sons. The mansion she died in is rumored to be haunted by the eerie sounds of a piano playing when there is supposedly no one home. It is also said that visitors often claim to experience unexpected cold chills and an eerie feeling in the basement area of the home. Does the spirit of Mrs.

The interior of the elaborate Rucker Bank, then located at 1602 Hewitt Avenue in Everett. It was a grand design with intricately carved wood, beautiful marble, fancy wallpapers and decorative counters. *Everett Public Library, photographer George Kirk.*

Rucker regret her decision? Is that why she refuses to leave the beautiful home? Why did a woman who seemingly had it all leap to her death? In 1923, the brothers sold the gorgeous Everett Mansion to Clyde Walton, a local lumber dealer, for just $32,500. That is almost $8,000 less than it originally cost them to build it. The brothers probably sold the house to Walton at such a low price because the memories of their mother's death were too painful. Walton and his family lived happily in the home until his death in 1959.

The brothers continued to prosper after their mother's death, and in 1921, they began building the impressive three-story Big Four Inn in Darrington, twenty-five miles east of Granite Falls. The project cost them $150,000 and consisted of fifty-three rooms located near the ice caves at the base of the mountains. Tourists came from all over to enjoy the Inn until it suffered a fire in the early hours of September 7, 1949.

The Rucker family continued to experience tragedy throughout the generations. Years after Jane Rucker's death, Margaret, the daughter of

The lovely poet, Margaret Rucker (daughter of Bethel Rucker), and her handsome husband, Justus Armstrong, both suffered from personal tragedy and sadly died by suicide. *Jason Webley and "Chicken" John Rinaldi.*

Bethel and Ruby Rucker, and her husband, Lieutenant Justus Armstrong, both died by suicide. Margaret was born in 1907 and was an extremely beautiful poet who studied at the University of Washington. She soon met the very handsome Justus and married him on July 16, 1931. They lived at 2601 Hoyt Avenue while in Everett. Years later, forty-six-year-old Justus died from a self-inflicted gunshot wound on April 21, 1950, in the den of their home in Burbank, California. The heartbroken Margaret died nine years later from an overdose of sleeping pills on June 18. Some wonder if the sad and brutal death of their firstborn son, John Wyatt, who lived only one day, could have led to the couple's suicides. Others believe Justus's depression from war was the culprit for his death. Tragedy can be created by many things, and most can never be understood by outsiders.

One strange coincidence in their deaths is a poem Margaret wrote during her college years titled "Two Deaths." It somehow predicted her and her husband's untimely death. Could Margaret foresee her future, or was she simply writing an innocent poem?

Jason Webley, a musician and songwriter, has produced several albums, including *Margaret*, an album based on the life of Margaret Rucker. His friend, "Chicken" John Rinaldi, found a scrapbook in a dumpster in San Francisco that contained photos of Margaret and her family. Years later, he and Jason came together to develop the wonderful *Margaret* project, which combined live performances of the album with images from the scrapbook. Images of Margaret and Justus, her husband, can be found on their website.

A story from Jason Webley, musician and songwriter:

> *I haven't seen the photos from inside the tomb, but I have been in there! A few years back, Bill Rucker had the tomb opened to show it to Margaret's grandchildren, who contacted me because of the project. They live in the Bay Area and visited. Not sure how complete the project is, but I have a handful of stories about the tomb, a couple of which are a bit "ghost" ish...*

NOTE: The Rucker mansion is a private residence; please do not disturb the owners or their property in any way. The mansion is occasionally open during the Historic Everett Home Tours, and many images can be found online for the curious. The Rucker mausoleum should also be respected and treated accordingly.

3

THE EVERGREEN CEMETERY AND THE RUCKER MAUSOLEUM

Our forefathers looked upon nature with more reverence and horror, before the world was enlightened by learning and philosophy, and loved to astonish themselves with the apprehensions of witchcraft, prodigies, charms, and enchantments. There was not a village in England that had not a ghost in it, the church-yards were all haunted, every large common had a circle of fairies belonging to it, and there was scarce a shepherd to be met with who had not seen a spirit.
—Joseph Addison, The Spectator

The Evergreen Cemetery was established in 1898 and has about fifty thousand interesting souls resting in it. The original plat was bought by the Everett Land Company and consisted of one hundred acres. The bodies of governors, congressmen, legislators, mayors, policemen, veterans, murder victims, victims from the 1910 Wellington avalanche and disaster, slaves, Everett's first undertaker and even President Obama's great-great-great-grandmother Rachel Wolfley reside there. It is even said that a local man was buried with his beloved sofa. The cemetery has also been a location shot for several movies including the Warner Bros. film *Assassins*, starring Sylvester Stallone and Antonio Banderas.

On the property, downhill from the thirty-foot-tall Rucker tomb stands a gazebo where pallbearers and coffins would wait during funeral processions. The cemetery is filled with western red cedar trees and several spikey monkey trees, which are said to ward off evil spirits.

David Dilgard from the Everett Public Library explains why these trees were planted through the cemetery:

> *The Native Americans in this region respected these trees as they were symbols of life and death. The red cedar was used for building housing and canoes, its bark used for clothing, and other parts were used for medicine. Upon death, a Snohomish tribesman would be lifted up high into a red cedar tree—often in a cedar box or basket. The tree formed an integral part of the Native Americans' lives. The red cedar also served an important role in the City of Everett's economy. Everett was, at one point, the largest producer of red cedar shingles anywhere in the world. These trees can be found throughout Evergreen Cemetery.*

Harry Tracy Continues to Wander

Harry Tracy (1875–1902) or one of his victims, Deputy Sheriff Charles Raymond (1859–1902), who's buried there, might be haunting the Evergreen Cemetery. However, even if it is Tracy's ghost, he was much more frightening in real life. From the day he escaped the Oregon State Penitentiary to the very hour of his death, Tracy left a trail of blood everywhere he went and killed eight men. His legacy can be summed up in this quote from the *Seattle Daily Times*: "In all the criminal lore of the country, there is no record equal to that of Harry Tracy for cold-blooded nerve, desperation and thirst for crime. Jesse James, compared with Tracy, is a Sunday school teacher."

Tracy's taste for crime started in the year 1897, when he was the leader of the Powder Springs Gang in Colorado. It is said that Tracy ran around with the world-famous criminal Butch Cassidy. In his early days, Tracy committed many robberies and participated in many gun fights, which soon landed him in the Aspen Colorado Jail. His incarceration didn't last long, and he escaped from the prison in 1898. He was arranged to be tried for murder when he bound and gagged the sheriff and killed Deputy Valentine Hay before escaping. Alongside David Merrill, his partner in crime, Tracy was arrested in Portland, Oregon, on February 6, 1899. Merrill testified against Tracy, which got him only thirteen years of prison time while it got twenty for Tracy.

Tired of life in prison, Tracy and Merrill, in the early hours of June 9, 1902, somehow acquired rifles and quickly took control of the prison.

A lifetime prisoner, Frank Ingraham, tried in vain to disarm the men but was eventually shot by Merrill. Tracy then shot the two prison guards: Frank Ferrell and Thurston Jones Sr. As they fled, they shot Bailey Tiffany, another guard, and used his body as a shield as they headed for the woods. Once they were under the cover of the trees—they brutally killed Tiffany.

After their escape, the outlaws traveled together for some time—holding up farmers along the way, demanding food, clothing and shelter. After the men slept in a graveyard one night, Tracy forced four men to take them on a ten-hour boat ride through the Puget Sound. The police learned of Tracy's plan, and he was eventually followed by Sheriff McKay and his men in an electric tugboat called the *Sea Lion*. However, by the time they started tracking Tracy, they already had a fifteen-hour head start on the men.

On July 3, 1902, Tracy fought with a posse of policemen in Everett, where he killed Deputy Sheriff Charles Raymond, E.E. Bresse and Neil Rawley. He also wounded two reporters before escaping once again. Tracy soon found shelter in the home of Charles Gorrell in Renton, Washington, on July 10. As another posse surrounded the man's home, Tracy was able to escape again as he ran into the bushes. The posse let loose some bloodhounds with which they were able to track Tracy for some time until he managed to sprinkle cayenne pepper on a boathouse, which put the dogs in agony and allowed Tracy to escape yet again.

Merrill is said to have reconnected with Tracy in Benton, Washington, but sometime after their reunion, the men quarreled, and a duel was set up on June 28, 1902. The desperate Tracy played unfairly and shot Merrill in the back of the head before leaving him to die in the woods of Napavine, Washington. The police found his body on July 16, and a statewide manhunt for Tracy ensued. During this time, Tracy trekked hundreds of miles until he landed on a farm in Creston, Washington, where he was once again pursued by a local posse of four men guided by Sheriff Gardener. His long crime spree ended

The notorious and ruthless outlaw Harry Tracy killed this Everett policeman, Charles Raymond (1859–1902), on July 3, 1902. Raymond is buried in the Evergreen Cemetery. *Deborah Cuyle.*

This mugshot of Harry Tracy is from a newspaper from 1902. One of his victims, Charles Raymond, is buried at the Evergreen Cemetery. *Everett Public Library, scanned from a photographic slide.*

at a place called Eddy's Ranch near Fellowes Railway Station, about fifty miles west of Spokane. He had been shot in the thigh and right leg, and he knew he would not be able to escape. Tracy used his last bullet on himself, and the famous outlaw was dead at age twenty-seven.

Interestingly, while Tracy's body was on display, gawkers began stripping it of clothing scraps, hair and other things as souvenirs. Once his body was isolated from viewers, its appearance was altered in order to deter people from later digging it up to be used as some sort of creepy, underground outlaw exhibit.

A ghost story from Lilly:

I used to roam the grounds [of] the cemetery in Everett when I was younger with [one of] my friends. It is a very beautiful place during the day, but at evening, we used to scare the wits out of each other! I would hide behind trees and she would have to find me. One time, I was waiting for her to find me and there was a man about ten feet away from me. I wanted to signal him to stay quiet so as to not give my location away. No sooner did I see him than he was gone—vanished! He was wearing strange clothes, like the kind from an old movie, and had a very thick moustache and black hat. To this day, I often wonder if it was the ghost of someone buried there. I didn't find the cemetery much fun after that, more frightening.

Could the ghost Lilly saw be the restless spirit of Tracy's gunshot victim, Charles Raymond? He is buried at Evergreen Cemetery and has every right to want to haunt from the grave. His young daughter Winnie, at only fourteen years old, died by suicide in Everett after swallowing carbolic acid. Perhaps the death of her loving father was just too much pain to bear. However, it is hard to say, since both men, when they were alive, matched the description Lilly gave.

THE SPIRIT OF OLE NELSON

While Tracy and Raymond are strong possibilities for spirit activity, the ghost in the cemetery could also be Ole Nelson, who was ruthlessly murdered in 1898 on the corner of Hewitt and Wetmore Avenues. Nelson also wore a thick moustache while alive. Several other people who were involved in this murder are now also resting at the Evergreen Cemetery, including Tomas Flemming, the man who tried to break up the fight, and Edward Dwyer, the sheriff and arresting officer. Are they watching over Ole Nelson's grave at the Evergreen Cemetery even after death?

From David Dilgard's notes:

> *Ole Nelson rests in an unmarked grave in the oldest section of Everett's Evergreen Cemetery. If you enter by the picturesque lych gate in the northeast corner of the graveyard, his resting place is directly before you. He lies in Lot fifty-seven of Block six, which cost $7.50 and was paid for by Everett Lodge #98 of the Knights of Pythias. The absence of any monument or marker makes locating the gravesite a bit tricky. It's a short distance from the lych gate at the northeast corner of the cemetery, a few feet west of a monument that somehow evokes melancholy irony with the inscription: Joy.*

The confrontation between Nelson and James Connella, the man who shot him, occurred on October 10, 1898. The bleeding Nelson was carried into the Commercial Hotel, then moved to a hospital on Broadway where four physicians struggled to save him. Doctors attempted surgery to repair the damage, but at half past midnight, Ole Nelson breathed his last breath.

The street where the confrontation between Nelson and Connella occurred on October 10, 1898. *Everett Public Library, David Dilgard Collection.*

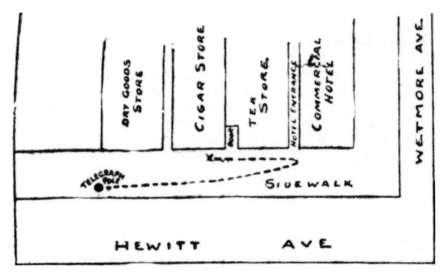

This map was drawn to indicate where the confrontation between Nelson and Connella occurred and, ultimately, where Nelson's body fell in front of Haferkorn's Cigar store. *Everett Public Library, David Dilgard Collection.*

William Haferkorn was a popular cigar merchant who opened his first store in 1897. This is his tombstone, with beautifully carved stone oak leaves, at the Evergreen Cemetery. *Everett Public Library, David Dilgard Collection.*

SNOHOMISH COUNTY, WASHINGTON, FRIDAY, OCTOBER 14, 1898.

SHOT

Ole Nelson Cold in Death

KILLED BY EDITOR CONNELLA

Quarrel Grows Out of the Charge by Connella That Nelson Tore Down the Picture at the Republican County Convention.

About seven o'clock Monday night, those in the vicinity of Haferkorn's cigar store in Everett were startled by loud words, a scuffle and then a pistol shot. James W.

A SPECIAL EDITI

A Tribune Enterprise That si couraged by Our peo

Two representatives of the T at Seattle have effected an with the TRIBUNE to issue a l edition of this paper on or ab inst, containing a concise state resources of Snohomish count business review of the city of the object of the special edit influence capital and immigrat This special edition will mak medium to send to eastern fri quirers in any part of the count present the resources of the city state of trade, price of land a mention of the principal indu gies houses and representative c

Mr. Lewis, in Everet Congressman Lewis was a speak in Everett last Monday a number of the Snohomish ho

This newspaper article from October 14, 1898, tells of the cold-blooded murder of Ole Nelson by an Everett newspaper editor, James Connella. *From the* Snohomish County Tribune.

William Haferkorn was a popular cigar merchant who opened his first store in 1897 on the corner of Hewitt and Wetmore Avenues, and he was mentioned as a witness in an article in the *Snohomish County Tribune*, October 14, 1898:

About seven o'clock Monday night, those in the vicinity of Haferkorn's cigar store in Everett were startled by loud words, a scuffle and then a pistol shot. James W. Connella, editor of the Everett News, *and Ole Nelson, a wood and coal dealer, met and in a quarrel which followed, Connella pulled his revolver and shot Nelson in the groin, the wound proving fatal. Deputy Sheriff Dwyer was nearby, and immediately took Connella in charge and to the jail. The deceased was generally known as a peaceful and law abiding citizen, and the citizens of Everett greatly deplore the fatal affair.*

The *Bismarck Daily Tribune* wrote on January 5, 1899:

J.W. Connella was cleared of the charge of murdering Nelson as he had knocked Connella down and beat him with a club and Connella therefore shot him back in self-defense.

Unfortunately, local citizens shunned Connella from the community, and he soon left town, never to be heard from again. Perhaps he haunts Everett in revenge of being displaced after he claimed to be just defending himself?

THE GRANDEST TOMB IN THE CEMETERY

The Rucker mausoleum was constructed in 1909 for Jane Morris Rucker (1830–1907) by her sons, Wyatt J. Rucker (1857–1931) and Bethel J. Rucker (1862–1945). This granite pyramid is thirty feet square by thirty feet tall and sits on a stone platform. It was designed and constructed from Washington granite by F.W. Ladd of Seattle at a cost of $30,000. The chapel space inside measures nine feet by twelve feet and has twenty-two crypts made from barre granite brought in from Vermont. The impressive pyramid sits seventy feet higher than the beautiful lych gate entrance.

The tomb boasts interesting windows and a heavy red beach granite door that measures four feet by seven feet and is four inches thick. The door can be opened by a large skeleton key that only the cemetery retains in its possession. It is rumored that when the mausoleum is opened, its massive door swings elegantly and effortlessly as if it is light as a feather—engineering at its finest in 1909! The inscription on the door is, "The pioneer of Everett, The true wife, The perfect mother, The soul of honor," and the inner walls of the tomb carry the names of the individuals who are resting peacefully inside.

Local stories tell of how the large slabs of granite were pulled up to the cemetery on temporary "train tracks" that were positioned specifically to make the job of pulling these massive stones easier for the horses. The tracks supposedly started down near the beautiful lych gate by the highway and led up to the present-day site of the tomb. The enormous blocks of granite were carved and placed on site—an incredible task even to this day!

Outside, the four corners of the Rucker mausoleum have large circles cut from them. Through these holes, three of the corners still host mature holly trees. The Celtic meaning of holly deals with the ruling of wintery realms with style, dignity and honor even in the midst of great challenge. The ancient Druids called the plant "the one the sun never forgot" since it was the only plant that remained green in the winter months. Holly is said to represent personal sacrifice in order to gain something of greater value. Jane Rucker was certainly thought of as a dignified and strong pioneer woman who made many sacrifices during her long trek to Port Gardner with her two boys. The holly trees have been there so long that groundskeepers fear the century-old roots threaten the base of the tomb, but the removal of the holly trees would be tragic.

A story from Collen DeCamillo of Everett:

[My friend and I] *both went to the tomb to just take a look around it. We weren't allowed inside, of course. However, we sat at the door, and I turned on my little voice recorder to see if anyone was* [there] *with us. It was a clear day with a slight breeze, and the cemetery* [is] *close to a highway, so we had a lot of background noise, but we were patient and tried to communicate anyway. We asked a few questions, gave* [the spirits] *time to answer, asked a few more, then decided to walk around and look at the structure. My friend had found an old picture of this amazing structure and noticed that something was missing. There may have been a statue of Jane Rucker on*

The top of the Rucker tomb can be seen from the top of the hill while driving by. In this photograph, the limbs of the tree appear almost spider-like in their placement in front of the tomb. *Deborah Cuyle.*

47

the top of the door frame, [but] now, it is gone. The groundskeeper climbed up and saw there were two holes that had bolts in them at one time, so we wondered, did it get stolen? Was it ever put there? Just as we were walking away, I felt a funny breeze on my neck [that] *blew my hair a little. I turned around just in time to see a white mist with a much-defined human shape walk right into the tomb! I stopped and yelled to my friend, "Hey, look!" But, it was too late…the ghostly shadow was gone.…I believe that it was Jane herself kind of thanking us for being concerned, or maybe she just wanted to make her presence known. I didn't get anything on the recorder due to all the background noise, but from time to time, I heard what sounded like a breath or female whisper. Could it* [have been] *someone trying to respond?*

When the mausoleum was built, it was proposed to include a large bronze statue of Jane Rucker herself over the doorway (as seen in the postcard). However, the statue has either long since disappeared or was never created and placed over the entrance. On the top of the slab, where this statue was supposed to sit, there are two bolt holes, which suggest that the statue did exist. Another tomb photo, taken at a later date and posted by a fan on Jason Webley's website, shows six long pegs sticking out of the top where the statue

This image from the *Reporter*, 1909, depicts a bronze statue of Jane Rucker above the entrance to the mausoleum. Although no statue exists today, the remains of the attachments are there. *Everett Public Library.*

would have been. Although the bolts and pegs do not solve the mystery of the whereabouts of the infamous statue, they do affirm the fact that the statue was most likely there at one point and that the slab was constructed to hold it. Some have suggested that the statue was melted down during World War I, but that theory is hard to believe.

A ghost story from the author:

> *We were at the Rucker mausoleum for a photography session when we decided to put a tape recorder near the large, granite door* [at] *the entrance. We proceeded to ask questions* [of] *Jane Rucker and her family, who* [are] *entombed inside. Although we did not hear any responses at the time of recording, we did hear a woman's voice when we played it back! It sounded like a woman whispering, but we could not make out the words as the traffic noise was too loud. Could this have been the spirit of the adventurous Jane Rucker herself? I would like to think that such a courageous and amazing woman would never want to leave her beloved town of Everett! I find it interesting that from the entrance side of her tomb, the "Everett" sign can be seen clearly from the mausoleum, almost as if she is still guarding her town.*

For those who are interested, the following is a list of those resting in the Rucker Mausoleum.

- Jane Morris Rucker, the beloved mother and for whom the tomb was originally built for by the Rucker brothers (Wyatt and Bethel), January 29, 1830–November 10, 1907.
- Wyatt Rucker, Jane's husband, who died on May 27, 1878, and was originally buried in Ohio before he was moved to Washington and placed in the Rucker tomb in 1929.
- Bethel J. Rucker, August 11, 1862–March 28, 1945, son of Jane and Wyatt Rucker.
- Wyatt J. Rucker, December 18, 1857–November 13, 1931, son of Jane and Wyatt Rucker.
- Ruby Brown Rucker, Bethel's wife, February 9, 1881–January 4, 1972, and for whom the haunted Rucker mansion was built.
- Jasper L. Rucker, Bethel's son, January 24, 1906–February 13, 1963.
- Margaret Rucker Armstrong, Ruby and Bethel's daughter, December 12, 1907–June 18, 1959, who died by suicide.

The Rucker mausoleum is a well-known Everett landmark that is located in the Evergreen Cemetery, perched high on the hill. The gigantic stones were moved to the location by horsepower and rolled on temporary tracks from the lower gazebo area. *Deborah Cuyle.*

- Justus Rogers Armstrong, Margaret's husband, May 16, 1904–April 21, 1950, who also died by suicide.
- John Wyatt Armstrong, Margaret's newborn son, January 18–19, 1936.
- Gertrude Rucker, Bill Rucker's mother, February 7, 1904–February 2, 2004.
- Susie Rucker, Bill Rucker's wife, May 18, 1940–July 2, 2009.

There are eleven spaces left inside the tomb and only one remaining family member, Bill Rucker, who states he will probably join his family when his time comes.

NOTE: Please be respectful and do not disturb, climb on or damage the Rucker mausoleum. The monument has unfortunately experienced destruction due to vandalism and unwanted litter in the past, so it is now under surveillance. The mausoleum is off limits after dark for these reasons.

4
TRINITY EPISCOPAL CHURCH

The ghostly realm can be just as real as our physical one; the specters are often quite ordinary people, living their busy lives alongside our own. They are like neighbors we are aware of, catching glimpses of them from time to time, hearing the odd sound from their part of the house, finding evidence they have just gone on ahead of us, slammed the gate and dashed off on their all-absorbing errands.
—*Paul Gater,* The Secret Lives of Ghosts

The idea of a new Episcopal church bloomed in the very early years of Everett's history when a group of people residing at the Bay View Hotel decided they needed one. So, in 1892, when Everett's population was around four thousand strong, the plan to build a new church began to take place. A Seattle reverend, James Cheal, traveled north to hold the town's first service in an old store. The members of the congregation knew that the church needed more space, so the generous Everett Land Company gifted four lots of land to the group at the corner of California and Wetmore Streets. The Trinity opened its doors in August 1892, and the salary for its reverend was $75 a month. When the eager Reverend Rogers took over in 1911, he paid his own salary for the first six months. In 1912, the church purchased three new lots at the corner of Twenty-Third Street and Hoyt Avenue for $4,500 and decided the new building would be designed by Ellsworthy Story. In 1920, a new section of the building was designed by E.T. Osborn with its Victory Memorial cornerstone.

The majestic Trinity Episcopal Church, located at 2301 Hoyt Avenue, was built to replace a much smaller church that was originally built in 1892. The church is adorned with gorgeous Tiffany-style milk glass fixtures, a pipe organ and a spectacular stained-glass window that was shipped to Everett from New York on a steamer, which was a very long journey since it was before the creation of the Panama Canal. Church officials today are very careful with the glass, because it is part of the original building, and the red-colored pieces can no longer be replicated.

Here are some more details from Pastor Rachel Taber-Hamilton's research:

This church's cornerstone was laid down just prior to the start of WWI. When the First World War began, work was halted as the working men of Snohomish County and many of its clergy went off to join the war effort. When the war was over, the building was completed in 1921 and dedicated as a WWI Victory Memorial to the brave men and women of Snohomish County [including members of the parish] *who had given their lives during the war. It was dedicated on Trinity Sunday in 1921 by Reverend Edgar Martin Rogers. It is a replica of St. Andrew's Church in Scotland in the tradition of classic church architecture. The stained glass above the altar, on the east wall, was created by Charles Connick of Boston. It is said that during transport of the glass to Everett, it was displayed in many cities. Connick's studio produced glass in a traditional Arts and Crafts way, and* [it] *was one of the most famous* [studios] *in America. His stained glass is in thousands of churches, including St. Patrick's Cathedral in New York and numerous other cathedrals. A contemporary of Tiffany, he preferred the style of medieval stained glass* [like that in] *Chartres Cathedral, France, where he studied the art.*

The original church was dismantled to make room for the $183,000 parish hall. The famous Reverend Edgar Rogers began his highly acclaimed youth program in the original church, so the new hall, designed by his son, John Rogers, a well-respected Seattle architect, was dedicated to him and serves as his memorial. The new hall is also said to be haunted by the wonderful and well-loved Reverend Edgar Rogers, who served as rector from 1911 until his death in 1941. In his time at the church, he grew its attendance as the town of Everett grew. It was through his hard efforts and determination that the church was built. Rogers Hall was completed in 1961 and can hold four hundred people in its main auditorium. The hall also holds a large, athletic-sized court on the main floor that's now used for large gatherings. Below the court is a fallout shelter with meeting rooms, a choir room and classrooms.

The church still remembers Reverend Rogers on their website:

> *During the first twenty years of its life, Trinity saw sixteen rectors come and go, but the Reverend Edgar Rogers broke this pattern of short tenures by serving as rector from 1911 to 1941.*

As for the ghost of Reverend Rogers, in his lifetime, he was a very honorable and generous man who devoted all of his energy to the church and Everett's townspeople. He gladly walked or rode his bike to make house calls for those in need. In 1916, after the war, Everett experienced a tragic Spanish flu epidemic that affected almost one hundred citizens, as reported by the *Everett Herald*, and Rogers comforted many of them. Since the church was such a huge part of his life, it is not wonder that Rogers wants it to be a huge part of his afterlife.

Kelly DiCicco, the parish administrator, told me that multiple friendly ghosts haunt his church. He says they all appear to be harmless and sometimes even a little mischievous:

> *We actually have several spirits that roam the various sections of the church. Father Rogers is the most active, as he tends to walk around the entire church. He is spotted quite often in the Columbarium* [a place for the storage of cinerary urns]…*because that area used to be his office when he was rector here. Another spirit is that of a man, we don't know his name, but he is heard and felt in our St. Luke's side chapel. A third ghost resides downstairs, and it is that of a youth named Adam. We know* [his name] *because White Noise Paranormal did an investigation and the name, Adam, was presented to them. We do not know what dates he was alive or why he is here. Adam stays in our Sunday School area, and I think he likes to pick on me the most! He likes to play games with me, like closing the doors or turning the lights off and on. He closes the door so much that I actually wrapped a brick in foil and wrote his name on it to put in front of the door to stop it from closing on me! He seems playful, and I talk to him when I am down there. A fourth ghost is that of a little girl* [that] *we have heard singing Sunday school songs. She is also downstairs and stays in the area of the prayer circle in the Sunday school. Another female spirit is here that is an adult. Her EVPs have been captured, and she is either singing or giving instructions. It is hard to tell.*

The Trinity Church and pews hold more than just confessions, prayers and sermons. It is said that the ghostly apparitions of five spirits walk the halls and rooms of the majestic building. *White Noise Paranormal.*

The beautiful Trinity Episcopal Church was built to replace a much smaller church that was built in 1892. It is said to be haunted by the wonderful and well-loved Reverend Edgar Rogers, who served as rector from 1911 to 1941. *Deborah Cuyle.*

Since there is no proof that the spirit is in fact Reverend Rogers, some speculate that the spirit could be another Trinity reverend or a member of the church. The members were also very involved in the community while they were alive, so that may explain why their spirits still roam around town. Proof of their involvement can be found in David Dilgard's notes:

> *On September 6, 1973, Mayor Bob Anderson and Everett police chief, Ed Sylte, announced the creation of a Police Department Chaplain Bureau during an Everett Ministerial Association Luncheon. Known unofficially as "the God Squad," the program recruited ten chaplains from different faiths to assist police and the public "during times of severe stress." On-call chaplains were identified with uniforms that clearly identified them as clergy.*

5
EVERETT COMMUNITY COLLEGE LIBRARY

Now it is the time of night, that the graves, all gaping wide…Everyone lets forth his sprite, in the church-way paths to glide.
—William Shakespeare, A Midsummer Night's Dream

T he library at Everett Community College (EvCC) in the Student Union Building offers more than just an excellent selection of reading materials and helpful staff. It is also the home of some friendly spirits that continue to enjoy the library every day. Many visitors to the library report seeing apparitions, feeling cold drafts, sensing a spirit nearby and other pleasant hauntings. Although no one really knows who the spirits are that reside here, we do know that they must be interested in reading. Could the ghosts who roam the halls be former students that cannot leave their beloved school? Or could the restless spirits be from another generation, possibly from a building that existed prior to the completion of the college? While some people have tried to contact the spirits for more information through drumming circles and other forms of spiritual communications, nothing has been made clear. Until the ghosts provide us with their names, the mystery will remain.

A story from Jeanne Leader, EvCC dean of arts and learning resources:

I have been at the library for twenty-two years now. Sometimes, people used to ask me, "What's with the guy at the desk," when there is no one there. They apparently saw a person sitting at the former location of the reference desk. The only thing I, personally, have experienced [was the flickering of the lights] *in one of the office areas after the library had closed and*

Many employees, students and visitors experience ghostly activity in the location of the previous reference desk at the Everett Community College library. *Deborah Cuyle.*

Staff members have seen ghostly apparitions sitting at these stations, sometimes seen as the partial figure of a male casually reading a book. *Deborah Cuyle.*

all [the] *other employees* [had] *gone. Years ago, I was part of an early morning drumming circle* [at the library], *and the leader of that activity said that she felt no negative energies present. All of them* [seem] *to be happy spirits that just love hanging out in our library!*

A story from Heather, an employee at Everett Community College:

At sunset, we went through the library with dowsing rods (two metal rods that "cross" when they encounter energy or water). Our most common sightings [at the library] *are near the old reference desk area,* [which is] *now under the "new books" sign. I* [have seen] *shades or forms around the library. One time, I saw part of a man's form sitting in a chair, just from the waist down, reading a book.*

A story from Laurie, an employee at Everett Community College:

I saw a form when I was investigating the library. I saw someone peeking around the corner.
    [That day,] *a group performed an early morning drumming circle and* [said] *there were no negative energies present....When we were* [investigating with] *the diving rods (also known as dowsing rods), about half way through the back area* [of the library,] *the rods crossed. I then saw a woman in her twenties, smiling at me—this was near the children's section. She was a white woman who had shoulder length dark hair. She was wearing dark colored pants, a shirt and a scarf. I also* [think] *I have a spirit that comes and checks on me occasionally* [when I am in the library]. *The male spirit is upstairs, on the third floor of the building. I experienced a spirit peeking through the windows* [there; it appeared] *to be* [an annoyed male] *who put his hands up against the window. There is no way an actual person* [could have done] *this as the area is too high up, and if anyone* [had been] *walking around out there* [I would have heard] *it. The spirits like to come to the door, too. A male co-worker* [of mine] *senses a female spirit in the library. His clock is always being knocked off the wall. The female spirit is also on the third floor of the building.*

6

THE EVERETT MASSACRE AND THE LABOR TEMPLE HAUNTINGS

The murdered do haunt their murderers, I believe. I know that ghosts have wandered on earth. Be with me always—take any form—drive me mad! Only do not leave me in this abyss, where I cannot find you!
—Emily Brontë

THE EVERETT MASSACRE

On November 5, 1916, one of the most horrific confrontations in Everett's history took place. Tensions rose between a local citizen's posse and members of the Industrial Workers of the World (IWW) union, also known as the Wobblies, until they broke in an event called the Everett Massacre.

In 1916, Everett was experiencing a depression, and to make matters worse, the local shingle workers had been on strike for almost half a year due to poor working conditions and "wage slavery." Around this time, the average wage in the Washington territory, per day with board, was $2.26. Shingles for roofs were in high demand during the time of the massacre, especially in Washington where the red cedar trees grew in abundance. The process for making these shingles was extremely dangerous; the workers had to move quickly and be very coordinated. These workers were considered highly skilled at the time and would produce, on average, fifty shingles per minute. However, this also meant that workers had to move their arms across sharp blades the same number of times per minute. These workers were

A reenactment of the Massacre in 1917 was orchestrated for the Oscar Carlson exhibit showing the *Verona* at the Everett City Dock where the deadly fight occurred. *Everett Public Library.*

offered no protection from the blades, and their bare arms were constantly exposed to the spinning blades. They were also exposed to fine dust that penetrated their noses, and "cedar asthma" quickly became a common condition among the men. Workers could always recognize a new shingle weaver by the fact that they still had all ten of their fingers. The tension was bound to grow as the men felt they deserved better working conditions and more pay. Thus, the strike began.

In order to support its nearby members, a large group of Seattle Wobblies boarded two steamers, the *Verona* and the *Calista*, and made their way north to offer their help with the public demonstration in Everett. This move did not go as planned, and opposing agencies met the *Verona* at the dock, demanding the Wobblies not disembark from the steamers. Local sheriff Donald McRae had organized a group of citizens to confront the striking workers. McRae had mixed reviews, as his practices were seen as somewhat brutal, reckless and unwarranted. An example of this can be found in how he treated a worker named Harry Feinburg. Feinburg was an organizer for the IWW

One of a series of postcards issued by the IWW in memory of Felix Baran, Hugo Gerlot and John Looney, three of the Wobblies killed in the Everett Massacre. Poet Charles Ashleigh is pictured giving the eulogy. *Everett Public Library.*

Oscar Carlson Exhibit photo showing the Everett City Dock, scene of the Everett Massacre, looking west from tug office with the steamer *Clatawa* behind the post in 1917. *Everett Public Library.*

who spoke occasionally on the corner of Hewitt and Wetmore in Everett to support the Wobblies right of free speech, and he was just twenty-five years old when he was cruelly beaten and jailed by Sheriff McRae. McRae was also known for the torment of an IWW prisoner named Earl Osborne, a logger from North Carolina who was the secretary in Everett's IWW office. After closure of the Everett IWW office in September 1916, Osborne was sent back to reopen it when he met the furious McRae, who quickly ran him out of town. McRae was also said to have pulled his pistol and hit men over the head with it on numerous occasions.

When the workers landed in Everett, McRae warned them, "You are not permitted to land! You cannot hold street meetings in Everett!" It was reported that one union man yelled back, "The hell we can't!"

Newspaper articles quoted Mayor Merrill of Everett saying:

> *We knew the IWWs were coming, and the committee was armed and waiting for them. When the steamer approached the dock, and before any lines were thrown out, Sheriff McRae stepped out. He asked for the leader and said he wanted to know what the party intended to do. There were 250 on the boat, I understand. "We're all leaders," they yelled.*

In 1917, this photograph of the *Verona* at the Everett City Dock was admitted as evidence in a suit filed by a man wounded during the massacre. The ship is shown in the position it occupied when the shooting started. The two Xs mark the spots where victims Beard and Curtis fell. *Everett Public Library.*

The pressure was on, and the mostly unarmed Wobblies confronted two hundred Everett citizens, who were under Sheriff McRae's charge. A single shot was fired, no one knows by whom, and for another ten minutes, gunfire was aimed in the direction of the *Verona*. Mayor Merrill told the newspaper, "A shot came from behind the smokestack. Many describe it was the first fired shot. There are people up there that say the men on the wharf fired first. I do not think this is so, though." Windows were shattered on the boat, and dozens of bullets riddled the woodwork. Four men fell with the first shots. Literally hundreds, some records indicate thousands, of bullets flew through the air as the frightened Wobblies quickly moved en masse toward the other side of the boat, nearly causing it to capsize.

Sheriff Donald McRae remains one of the central figures of the Everett Massacre. McRae suffered two minor shots to his legs during the shootout. *Everett Public Library.*

Many of the men were tossed into the cold waters and several drowned. The captain, Chance Wiman, somehow managed to steer his boat away from the dock and back to safety, where he then warned the crew on the *Calista* of the danger in Everett.

When the Wobblies were arrested, there were no guns found, and it was believed they were tossed into the water prior to their defeat. Among the men known to have held guns on board the *Verona* were Ed Roth, the "ringleader," Albert Scribner, John Berry, Robert Mulholland, who was just eighteen years old, and Dan McCarthy.

The death toll was recorded as two dead citizen deputies, five dead IWW members, but others suggest it was somewhere between twelve and twenty-seven, although some articles claim fifty were wounded. Despite this horrific event, the Everett Wobblies continued with their free speech demonstration on the corner of Hewitt and Wetmore Avenues. At this time, Everett had a street ordinance about speaking that allowed citizens to utilize the cross streets of Hewitt Avenue as long as they stayed fifty feet away from the thoroughfare. The Wobblies respected this and marked off exactly fifty feet.

Frustrated, Sheriff McRae and his men were soon hauling more of the workers off to jail. A total of 128 Seattle Wobblies were jailed for nine days before they were finally released on November 13. Three women

Oscar Carlson Exhibit photo of the Everett City dock, scene of the Everett Massacre, from the tug office with a car parked nearby in 1917. *Everett Public Library.*

who were in support the Wobblies, Lorna Mahler, Edith Frenette and Joyce Peters, were also arrested in connection with the massacre, and Judge Dikeman refused to release them. Frenette was released from her unlawful assembly charge on a bail of $1,000, but she soon got herself into more trouble when she attempted to shoot Sheriff McRae in a frenzy. The *Leavenworth Echo* wrote on November 10, 1916, that according to reports of eyewitnesses, Frenette attempted to shoot Sheriff McRae as he was driving past the crowd at the Great Northern tracks on his way to the hospital. A man knocked her gun out of her hand before she could shoot. Sheriff Donald McRae remains one of the central figures of the story of the Everett Massacre. While the Wobblies saw him as a villain, businessmen saw him as a protector. Elected on the Progressive Party ticket in November 1912, Donald McRae had an established, credible record as a labor advocate, having served actively in the shingle workers union.

Eventually, a union leader named Thomas H. Tracy was charged with the murders of the two citizen deputies: Snohomish County deputy

Top: Prisoner 4860, Tom Tracy, when he was booked on November 5, 1916. Tracy, a crane driver, was born in Pennsylvania and known as "Little Tom" Tracy. *Everett Public Library.*

Left: Prisoner 4866, Thomas H. Tracy (alias George Martin), was a teamster from Nebraska charged with killing deputy Jefferson Beard. Tracy was the first and only prisoner brought to trial in the Everett Massacre case. He was acquitted of murder after a brutal defense by attorney George Vanderveer. *Everett Public Library.*

sheriff Jefferson Beard and Lieutenant Charles Curtis of the National Guard. However, many witnesses claimed that the shots that killed the two men were actually fired from behind them, which means they were killed by their own men, *not* the Wobblies. Beard's wife forever carried a deep grudge against McRae, and she kept her deceased husband's bloody jacket as proof of his death by friendly fire, since it had a bullet hole in the back but not the front. Tracy was acquitted of the crimes on May 5, 1917.

Later, Mayor Merrill declared that he was warned that the Wobblies were going to burn Everett and kill McRae that day. When detectives questioned the injured union men on why they were coming to Everett, many simply replied, "To get free speech."

The five murdered Wobblies were Felix Baran, Hugo Gerlot, John Looney, Abe Rabinwitz and Gus Johnson. Hugo Gerlot was just twenty-two years old when he was killed. Other men said he sang the tune "Hold the Fort" as he

Jefferson Beard (1871–1916) began working as a log setter but soon became a Republican appointee to the Everett police force. He later worked as the county deputy sheriff. Beard was killed on the city dock on November 5, 1916. Charges were brought against seventy-four Wobblies for murdering Beard. *Everett Public Library.*

fell off the deck of the ship *Verona*. The poor young man was shot twice in the head, once in both arms, once in his hip and once his leg. The first verse of the song predicts the poor man's demise:

We meet today in Freedom's cause,
And raise our voices high;
We'll join our hands in union strong,
To battle or to die.

Felix Baran came from Illinois and was born to a shoemaker named Jozef and his wife, Victoria—both had immigrated to the United States from Germany. He was fatally shot in the abdomen and died later in the hospital from internal hemorrhaging.

Not much is known about John Looney except that he was a handsome young man.

The other two men, Gus Johnson and Harry Pierce, were listed among the dead in the newspapers. Abraham Rabinowitz was also listed among the dead, and it is said that he died while singing "The Red Flag." The same song was sung by mourners as they threw flowers upon the coffins of the men.

The first four lines of "The Red Flag" lyrics are:

The workers' flag is deepest red,
It shrouded oft, our martyred dead;
And ere their limbs grew stiff and cold
Their life-blood dyed its every fold.

These men came in peace and with the hopeful idea of speaking their minds, but tragedy followed and these young men lost their lives. After the massacre, some 468 IWW members showed up to march in the funeral procession alongside three hearses, each carrying the men who were to be buried at Mount Pleasant Cemetery, located at Queen Anne Hill in Seattle.

They dragged the river for quite some time, hoping to locate the drowned men, but none were ever recovered. Rumors were spread that the six to twelve bodies were secretly disposed of to avoid more tension, but official records indicate that only seven Wobblies were actually missing. These numbers were contested in court, and a quote from the *Seattle Star* on November 6, 1916 states:

That three to five victims fell off the steamer into the water after the opening volley was the opinion brought out in the inquest by conducted by Coroner A.R. Maulsby at Everett. "We have been dragging all morning but have been unable to locate any of the bodies. We are pretty certain there are more dead. The testimony has established that," said Maulsby.

Some of the photographs of the crime scene were admitted as evidence of additional deaths in a civil suit filed by a man wounded on the steamer *Verona* during the Everett Massacre. These "unrecovered," drowned and tragically shot men who lost their lives so senselessly that day were never properly buried or acknowledged, and they could be some of the ghosts that now reportedly haunt the Labor Temple in Everett.

Some of the other men who were notable during the time of the massacre were:

- Joseph Manning, prisoner 4889, age twenty-eight, was an automobile repairman from Pennsylvania. In his trial testimony, he said he was in the cabin with Thomas Tracy when firing began. He sought cover behind a smokestack where he was joined by Tracy.

- Jack Leonard, prisoner 4863, age twenty-seven, was a laborer from Kentucky. More widely known as Jack Miller, this defendant was the last known surviving *Verona* passenger until his death in 1986. A spirited and eloquent spokesman for the IWW until the end, Jack was frequently the subject of Seattle-area newspaper interviews and appeared in the documentary film called *The Wobblies*.
- James Whiteford (Kelly), prisoner 4873, age thirty-six, was a cook from New York. Whiteford, unfortunately, was wanted in Pennsylvania for a parole violation, and he was pressured to testify for the prosecution. When he refused, he was apparently extradited and served a long penitentiary sentence. The IWW praised him for his loyalty and his refusal to betray his fellow workers.
- Axel Downey, prisoner 4848, at the very early age of seventeen, was a laborer from Iowa. Downey was the youngest of the prisoners. It is said that he was pressured to make a statement but refused. He was referred to as a witness for the prosecution in order to "create distrust and suspicion among the prisoners."

THE LABOR TEMPLE

In 1909, the Everett Labor Temple members were proud to boast that they owned their building free and clear due to the collaborative efforts of some thirty different unions. The temple supported workers from every industry in Everett. Some of the biggest employers in town were the Pacific Steel Barge Company, which provided work for 135 men; Puget Sound Reduction company with 150 men; Puget Sound Pulp and Paper Company with 125 men; and the Smith Lumber Company, which employed 100 men.

The Labor Temple in Everett is said to be haunted, and the most probable culprits of this would be the frustrated and restless spirits from the 1916 Massacre. There are still many active labor disputes in Everett that the temple actively advocates for, which is likely the reason these union men are haunting it. Some statistics from the temple's website claim:

Several investigations have discovered restless spirits in the Labor Temple building at 2812 Lombard Avenue in Everett. Could they be the spirits of the young men who lost their lives during a labor dispute in 1916? *White Noise Paranormal.*

The Snohomish County Labor Council is a federation of sixty-three unions in Snohomish County. Those unions represent 42,000 working families for the purpose of bargaining wages/salaries and working conditions with their employers.

No wonder the Labor Temple might be haunted—the organization's goal is to protect employees from some of the exact same problems the Wobblies experienced in 1916. Could some of the shingle workers that were killed during the Everett Massacre be hanging around the Labor Temple in the hopes of helping today's hardworking Everett employees? A story from Raven Corvus of White Noise Paranormal:

At the Labor Temple in Everett, we have gotten recordings of a male voice on many occasions. We have investigated the location three times now. It's always pretty active. The people that work late in the building have had experiences, too.

7

THE HALLOWEEN MURDER
OF A LOCAL BAKER

For who can wonder that man should feel a vague belief in tales of disembodied
spirits wandering through those places which they once dearly affected, when he
himself, scarcely less separated from his old world than they, is forever lingering
upon past emotions and bygone times, and hovering, the ghost of his former self,
about the places and people that warmed his heart of old?
—*Charles Dickens,* Master Humphrey's Clock

Abook about ghosts in Everett would not be complete without the story
of the senseless killing of a young baker on a dark Halloween evening
in 1934. Although the crime unfortunately went unsolved for many
years, the perpetrator, Henri Young, finally confessed many years later while
serving time in the famous Alcatraz Island Federal Penitentiary.

A story from Sue C. in Lake Stevens;

> *I walk my dog in Everett with my friends, and we like to look at all the*
> *beautiful homes there.* [One of my friends] *was telling me some of*
> *the local* [ghost] *stories she has read about....One was of a murder on*
> *Halloween a long time ago off Colby Avenue. I don't know if she was*
> *pulling my leg or telling the truth, but she said, once, she* [smelled]
> *baked bread and even saw a ghostly image of a man on the sidewalk on*
> *Halloween night, the same day as the shooting of the baker a long time*
> *ago. There were other ghost stories but walking past the actual sight*
> *for this one was a little unnerving. It is weird to think about someone*

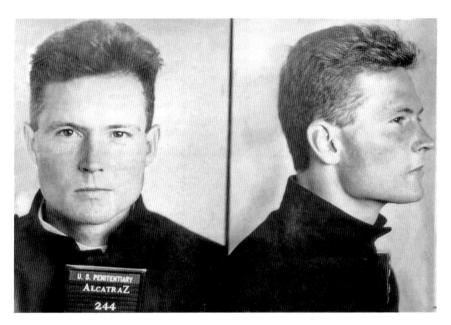

Henri Young was a bank robber, killer and kidnapper whose crimes eventually landed him in a cell at Alcatraz. He shot an Everett baker on Halloween night in 1934, and the spirit of his victim, William Buehrig, may still haunt the area. *Wikimedia Commons.*

losing their life at a certain spot and today it is as of nothing ever happened there. I wonder if that is why ghosts hang around a place—to be remembered.

Does the angry spirit of the innocent baker named William still walk Colby Avenue? When Buehrig moved his family to Everett in 1929 from Germany, he dreamed of a new life. He bought the bakery at 2101 Colby Avenue in 1932 from Mrs. Oden Hall to make dreams a reality for his new baby girl, Eleanor.

When the crime occurred that fateful night, there were few clues as to who the actual killer was. At the scene, there were a few spent slugs, a checkered cap that was knocked off the head of one of the criminals, a few neighbors' testimonies and the cash register tossed to the floor. The newspapers reported that the evidence revealed that a .32-caliber pistol was used at six o'clock on that night to rob the Colby Bakery.

It was expected that the killer entered the bake shop and William struggled with him as shots went off. Mrs. Buehrig was upstairs in their living quarters with her new baby when she heard the gun go off twice.

The baker on duty that night, Anton Burklund, was in the back room, busy preparing goods for the next day, when he heard some ruckus. He said he heard men demanding money but shrugged it off as a Halloween prank until he heard the gunshots. Policemen Jack Johnson and Clarence DeMars responded to the call and met William's frightened and grieving wife above the bakery. The Everett Ambulance Company was immediately called, but poor William had died almost instantly according to Coroner Challacombe.

After the incident, police combed the area, questioning locals. They were told by Mrs. William Kingshott, a neighbor, that earlier that night, she saw a light-colored sedan parked nearby in an alley off Twenty-First Street. On the same street, a policeman named Peter Clawson was parked near Wetmore. If it were not for noise of the heavy rain, Clawson may have been able to hear the gunshots. Neighbor James Bushfield, at 2104 Colby, was gardening that evening across the street when he saw two young men come around the corner then hesitate before entering the bakery. After the shooting, Kingshott said she saw a young woman meet them on the sidewalk before moving back to the alley. Was this unknown woman in charge of driving the getaway car? Her identity was never revealed. The police officers investigating the case attempted to follow all of the clues and several suspects, but they were never able to solve it.

After the tragedy Ellen Buehrig moved back to Germany in the hopes of rebuilding her life with her young daughter. Strangely, William's daughter contacted the Everett Library, where she discovered that the crime had finally been solved as she researched her family's history. She saw a photograph of Henri Young, the killer, finally putting a face to the crime. She read old newspaper articles on the murder. The horrible Halloween crime that destroyed her happy family so long ago was all over a mere ten dollars that Young found in the cash register.

How did the murder finally get solved? Almost a decade later, in 1943, while serving time in Alcatraz, Young confessed to the killing in a letter to Snohomish County prosecutor Leslie Cooper. Filed on March 24, 1944, the confession states:

> *On or about the thirty-first day of October, 1934…Henri Young did commit a crime of first degree murder while engaged in committing, attempting to commit, and in withdrawing from the scene of the crime of robbery with the premeditated design to effect the death of a human being, did willfully, unlawfully and feloniously then and there shoot*

at, toward and into the body of one William Buehrig…with a certain deadly weapon…a pistol then and there loaded with powder and ball…

Young went to trial but was not sentenced to death since he said he was studying to become a priest. In 1954, he returned to Washington to begin serving his life sentence for the killing of Beuhrig.

Young had a reputation for being a bank robber, burglar, kidnapper and killer, and he is considered to be one of the most intelligent criminals in history. While serving time in Alcatraz, Young continued to be a problem. In 1939, Young and several other famous inmates attempted to escape from Alcatraz. Young, Rufus McCain (who Young later stabbed to death), Dale Stamphill, Arthur "Doc" Baker and William Martin somehow managed to saw through iron cell bars in an isolation unit. The men quickly made their way to the water's edge but were caught by the guards. Three of the men surrendered, but Baker and Stamphill refused, so the guard shot them. Baker later died from his wounds.

In a statement filed by Prosecuting Attorney Cooper, he said, "I personally believe that the defendant is an extremely dangerous character. The physician's records of the United States Penitentiary at Alcatraz Island indicate that the defendant is partially criminally insane." When Young's parole came up in 1972, the sixty-two-year-old criminal left the prison, jumped parole and simply disappeared. In 1999, the state legally declared him dead.

The movie *Murder in the First*, starring Kevin Bacon, falsely depicts Young as a mistreated victim of false imprisonment. In reality, Young was a manipulative and conniving criminal and a ruthless killer. Does Henry's guilty soul roam Colby Avenue in Everett, perhaps regretful of the crime he committed in 1934?

NOTE: Please do not disturb the current business located at this site.

8

THE OLD YMCA BUILDING

A ghost is someone who hasn't made it—in other words, who died, and they don't know they're dead. So they keep walking around and thinking that you're inhabiting their—let's say, their domain. So they're aggravated with you.
—Sylvia Browne

HISTORY OF THE EVERETT FAMILY YMCA

Excerpts taken from "The First 100 Years," a pamphlet written by Lawrence E. O'Donnell (as given by Coleen Temple, Director of Marketing & Communications, YMCA of Snohomish County, Association Office).

The origins of the Everett YMCA can be traced to December 1899, when a group of men gathered in the side room of Everett's First Baptist Church. Being familiar with the YMCA movement, which had started in London in 1844, they wished to start their YMCA in Everett, a city which was less than ten years old.

On November 15, 1900, August Heide, the prominent designer of many early Everett buildings, presented drawings for a new YMCA building. The estimated cost was $3,426. The building would be erected on the northwest corner of Rockefeller Avenue and California Street. The lots, valued at $2,000, were donated by John McChesney and the Everett Improvement Company. Construction was finished in less than three months, and on the evening of Wednesday, May 1, 1901, approximately three hundred people assembled for the building's formal opening. It had taken less than seventeen months for the dream of a YMCA in Everett to become a reality.

On March 30, 1920, the YMCA building was seriously damaged by a fire, which would kick-start the organization into its most ambitious undertaking yet. By morning, word of the fire had spread throughout the community and leadership immediately decided to launch a campaign for a new building. The campaign began on April 19, and by April 26, $142,623 had been gained of the original $152,000 goal. The leadership teams regrouped to identify pledges. In the end, $183,598 was raised for the new Everett YMCA. The new building would be constructed at the same Rockefeller Avenue and California Street location, and additional lots were purchased for a much larger structure. The cornerstone was laid with formal Masonic ceremony on September 16.

On Sunday, April 10, 1921, the facility was officially dedicated. Described as formal Georgian style, the structure was four stories tall with a full basement. The basement included a swimming pool, locker rooms and showers. The first floor featured a community room and kitchen, two spacious lobbies, a library and various meeting rooms and offices. A gymnasium with a running track above, a handball court, a recreation room, three large classrooms and twenty-one dormitory rooms were among the second floor's features. The third and fourth floors contained a room for religious work programs, a large classroom and thirty-seven private dormitory rooms. This is the brick building that still stands today.

In January 1961, the new and remodeled facility was introduced to the community. Among the building's features was a new three-and-a-half-foot-deep training pool, refurbished dormitory rooms on the third and fourth floors of the 1920s building, a new businessman's lounge, a steam room, Hi-Y rooms, youth and adult lobbies and locker rooms and an additional gymnasium. In November 1977, the board approved a $2.9 million capital campaign for yet another building update. This plan would include a sixty-five-thousand-square-foot facility enhancement. With the nation gripped in high inflation spike, the campaign goal was changed to $4.2 million. In the summer of 1980, the YMCA had enough money to proceed with the project. In 1987, a new constitution was drafted, changing the name to the Young Men's Christian Association. While the Everett YMCA is the beginning of the YMCA in Snohomish County, the association expanded between 1964 and 2016, adding YMCA branches in Marysville, Mill Creek, Monroe, Mukilteo and Stanwood-Camano and affiliate Big Brothers Big Sisters of Snohomish County. The Everett YMCA will move into its new home at 4730 Colby Avenue in Everett in November 2019, leaving behind the history and stories from the corner of Rockefeller Avenue and California Street.

Hauntings of the Everett Family YMCA

Located on California Street and Rockefeller Avenue, the old YMCA building has long been known to be haunted. Locals and investigators feel that the spirit haunting the building belongs to a former janitor named George, who refuses to leave. The story goes that on March 30, 1920, a fire broke out in the original YMCA building, which was built in 1901 and located at 2720 Rockefeller Avenue. During the fire, it is said the brave janitor saved the lives of many children who were trapped inside, but he later died from the effects of the fire.

Today, at the YMCA, his voice apparently comes over the intercom and various equipment moves for no reason. It is said that the ghost of George can somehow make the heavy punching bag in the old gym move when no one else is in the room, just the eye of the camera. Other things that go bump in the night might be attributed to the fact that a section of the YMCA was once used as a hostel. This part of the building has been termed "ghost town," and pranksters have been known to splash red paint around the eerie place to imitate blood.

A ghost story as told by Pam Sipos, YMCA employee 1983–2010:

Some people believe there is a ghost that haunts the [Old] *YMCA.…He was nicknamed George in honor of YMCA founder, George Williams.* [My version of the] *story goes that there was a resident who lived on the fifth floor* [the fourth and fifth floor were dormitories for men until 1978] *who died in his room. No one knew he was in there until the smell became overwhelming. That is George. Over the years, some YMCA* [members] *who have stayed late or came in early* [have] *reported hearing George walking the halls and stairs, rattling things and* [flickering lights]. *Eve, who opened the YMCA at four am for many years, used to tell us about George* [sightings] *all the time. I have to admit, I spent many overnights at the YMCA but never heard or saw anything, but of course, I was surrounded by kids. I came in July of 1983 as the youth director. When school started that fall, a group of students from Everett High School descended on Ghost Town and went to work after school every day, preparing it for the annual Haunted House. That October I was amazed to see people lining up around the block on nights* [when the Haunted House was] *open. A number of people complained to me about having a haunted house at the YMCA, so the following year, I went up* [to Ghost Town] *when* [the students] *arrived. They were tearing out walls, painting "blood" over everything and creating macabre scenes of murders. I also saw students smoking—with an exposed lathe and litter everywhere! I also didn't think haunted houses belonged in the YMCA, but the smoking was breaking the rules and extremely dangerous, so I petitioned that they couldn't come back. That was the end of the Haunted House. Soon after, a group of staff went up to Ghost Town with a few pastors and we blessed every room with holy water and painted over the scary stuff.*

A ghost story from Christie E. in Everett:

A ghost affectionately known as George haunts the YMCA. One of the gals in the KidZone told me that during nap-time, she had a little one who was talking to someone who wasn't there. When asked about it, the kid said she'd been talking to George.

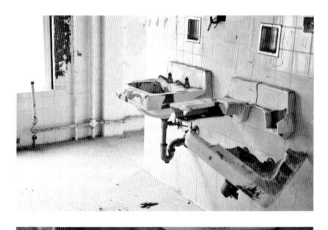

Artificial "bloody" sinks are found in the old YMCA building. Perhaps they were part of a prank or evidence of the hauntings in the building. *Richard Porter.*

The crumbling and peeling walls of the old YMCA building appear right out of a horror movie. An unknown woman lurks in the hallway, searching for ghosts. *Richard Porter.*

Richard Porter, a writer for *Live In Everett*, did a wonderful story on the YMCA's "Ghost Town," and he has graciously given me permission to reprint some of it for my book.

There is a dissonant feeling I always get at the Everett YMCA. It's the feeling of walking in a labyrinth, the feeling of climbing up a staircase with many doors and passages. Like a dream. Nowhere is this disorienting feeling more palpable than the chilly passages of the YMCA's "Ghost Town." Ghost Town is two floors of dormitories in the original 1920s building—one floor for ladies, the other for men. You have never seen Ghost Town because it is locked up. The floor is littered with crumbled plaster, peeled wallpaper, and discarded brochures. Each floor of Ghost Town has about thirty rooms that line narrow corridors. The dormitories have internal interconnecting doors that have been removed. You're never quite sure where one room ends and another begins. I kept turning around to discover another drafty passage behind me. I saw abandoned kitchens with vintage refrigerators left ajar, old shower rooms with cracked tile, and jumbled piles of discarded chairs. Some of the rooms have great views of the cityscape and the Cascade mountains. Other rooms are windowless, dark, and shoved full of cardboard boxes spilling glossy old YMCA camp photos. Ghost Town transports you to a different era, a time when you could arrive in Milltown and put down a few dollars for a room at the Y. A shower, a television, steam heat, an indoor pool, and a place to lay your head. Ghost Town was renovated in the 1960s and closed in 1978. I am not sure why it was closed. I can't seem to find a reason. The old building has been cut up many times for renovations, resulting in those confusing passages, random-seeming corridors and a few staircases that lead to nowhere. The closed dormitories of Ghost Town were used as a haunted house in the 1980s. There is graffiti on some of the walls, holes intentionally punched through the lathe and plaster, cracked sinks splattered in red paint to simulate blood. I'm not sure why this historic structure was turned into a corny teenage funhouse. The ultimate fate of Ghost Town is uncertain. The YMCA building at 2720 Rockefeller is now on the market. A new YMCA is being built in the Glacier View Neighborhood and is scheduled to be completed by the end of 2019.

9

THE EVERETT HIGH SCHOOL AUDITORIUM

I do believe in ghosts, or at least in some kind of persistent spiritual echoes of the past in certain places.
—Jennifer McMahon

I t is rumored that a spirit called the Blue Ghost roams the rooms of Everett High School, located at 2416 Colby Avenue. The story says that a man who was hired to renovate the auditorium fell to his death while working on the building. He broke his neck in the fall and continues to haunt the room. In the 1960s, many students and teachers reported seeing lights turning off and on by themselves and other strange sightings.

The new Everett High School opened on January 31, 1910. The three-story, Beaux Arts–style brick structure cost nearly $200,000 and housed nearly six hundred students. The building took up an entire city block and was designed by James Stephen, who designed other Washington buildings as well. The building's historic entry has lovely, wide corridors, with large stairs to accommodate the hundreds of students. The notes of David Dilgard contain more details about the school.

The [school] *building came at the end of a decade of growth that saw Everett's population triple. It was followed by the Vocational and Commercial buildings across the street,* [in] *1912 and 1915, respectively. Both were designed by Everett's Benjamin Turnbull. In 1940, the Civic Auditorium, designed by Earl Morrison, replaced the old Lincoln School.*

Does the restless spirit of a local worker still haunt the Everett High School auditorium where he fell and broke his neck? *Everett Public Library.*

A ghost story from Christie E.:

> *The auditorium at Everett High School is haunted. I actually read about this in a book...* [which claimed that the ghost is] *someone who died* [after] *falling off a ladder....* [They were] *working on lighting for a show* [at the school]....[In the auditorium, there are] *strange noises, lights* [turn] *on* [after they've] *been turned off, and mysterious faces appear in windows.*

10
OTHER EVERETT HAUNTS

"Not everybody believes in ghosts, but I do. Do you know what they are, Trisha?"
She had shaken her head slowly. "Men and women who can't get over their
past…That's what ghosts are."
—Stephen King, Needful Things

McCabe's American Café

The old dance club, called McCabe's American Café, was located at 3120
Hewitt Avenue in a building that is now used for offices. The building was an
investment of W.G. Swalwell, a pioneer developer of Everett's east side, with
Melvin Swartout. Melvin Swartout was born in Michigan and then moved
to Iowa until he and his wife, Maud, came out to the town of Everett to live.
Melvin started the Swartout Company at 2209 Rucker with W.G. Swalwell
acting as president. In its early days, the building served as a local spot for
Fourth of July events.

In the 1900s, there were two businesses listed in the building: Maud
Buckles Dressmaker and O.A. Phelps and Son Undertakers. Orville and his
son Guy were both funeral directors and embalmers, which is perhaps this
why the building is now haunted. In 1937, a man named Gus Kassionas
moved into the building. Kassionas was born in Greece in 1888. He boarded
the SS *Martha Washington* in Patras on September 4, 1909, with dreams of
coming to America. Soon after, he arrived in New York and didn't end up

Top: A group of hardworking men pose at the extended section of Swalwell's Dock, located at the foot of Everett Avenue, on March 10, 1892. *Bottom*: Early Everett with the train tracks rolling through town. Sign reads, "Watch out for cars." *Everett Public Library, King & Bakersville Collection and the Frank La Roche Collection.*

The former McCabe's American Music Café was located at 3120 Hewitt Avenue and was once a very popular dance club. *Deborah Cuyle.*

in Washington until 1920, when he made his move to Everett. He married Mary Stewart in March 1921, and their place of residence was listed as the upper floor of the McCabe building. There, he developed his dream of opening his own bar, which he called the Castle Bar. He lived in his new town of Everett until his death in 1958. He is buried at Cypress Lawn Cemetery.

The building continued for several decades as a tavern. It has now been lovingly restored to its full potential and is listed in the National Register of Historic Places.

A ghost story from paranormal investigator Raven Corvus:

> *We have investigated the building several times. We got some awesome EVPs there. My favorite one was of a woman* [who] *was close to the elevator* [and] *said, "Hello fellas!"* [The] *most famous haunting stories of McCabe's* [are always about] *music playing. When the owners were renovating the bar, they had shut the power off at one point. A few construction workers claim they heard a woman saying, "Here we go again," and then some old-time music started playing. The crew left and wouldn't go back for days.*

The dance floor in the former McCabe's American Café building was haunted by several ghosts, some of which appeared in mirrors and whispered things in people's ears. *White Noise Paranormal.*

A ghost story from Wendy:

> *I used to go dancing at McCabe's in Everett…before it closed, of course.…* *[Once,] I had a few drinks and was ready to dance, I but wanted to check my hair and makeup before I went out onto the floor. I went into the women's bathroom, and as I was looking into the mirror, I saw a woman behind me.…She did not look frightening.…She looked* [lonely] *to me and maybe even sad. She had dark hair and wore a fancy dress. She just stared at me. I did not move.…She disappeared as quickly as she appeared.…I wondered if she was a ghost of some woman who lived there a long time ago.*

A ghost story from a paranormal investigator, Raven Corvus of White Noise Paranormal:

> *The legend* [says] *that a woman of the night named Hanna was pushed down the stairs by an angry customer and died. Two of our investigators heard the music playing while they were investigating upstairs near the*

84

Right: This eerie carved figure of a cowboy once stood solemnly with a noose around his neck as decoration in the old dance club. *White Noise Paranormal.*

Below: Unknown men gather in front of the Swalwell Real Estate and Insurance building in 1892. W.G. Swallwell also owned Swalwell Land Loan and Trust company in Everett. *Everett Public Library.*

restrooms. They said it came out of nowhere, and they heard a woman sigh just before the old-time music started up. It only lasted a few seconds. [My sister-in-law and I] *were in the upstairs lounge doing an EVP session, when all of a sudden,* [we saw] *what we could only describe as a freight train coming at us....It was almost like we were being rushed at by an angry spirit.* Ghost Hunters *investigated the bar around 2006. The evidence they got was so freaky that the owner wouldn't allow them to air the episode. She was afraid it would scare off customers. She sold the bar and bought one in Mount Lake Terrace.*

NOTE: Please do not disturb the current business.

CATHOLIC COMMUNITY SERVICES BUILDING

A committed employee named Jerri, who loved her job and worked tirelessly at the center when she was alive, haunts the century-old brick building located at 1918 Everett Avenue. Reportedly, dogs in the building bark at nothing, bone-chilling drafts fill the rooms and other unexplained things go bump in the night. People have reported seeing Jerri's ghostly image fumbling for a cigarette and talking to herself. A supervisor said they once stopped in the building during the night when his dog began to bark nonstop and race up and down the hallway. Needless to say, both he and the dog left quickly! Is this really the spirit of Jerri, or could it be something else?

11
THE HAUNTED SHIPS OF EVERETT

In war, there are no unwounded soldiers.
—José Narosky

Some places speak distinctly. Certain dark gardens cry aloud for a murder; certain
old houses demand to be haunted; certain coasts are set apart for shipwreck.
—Robert Louis Stevenson

USS *FIFE*

Homeported in Everett, Washington, the Spruance-class destroyer USS *Fife* was in operation with the U.S. Navy from 1980 to 2003. The ship was named after Admiral James Fife Jr. (1897–1975), a submarine force commander during World War II. Its initial launch date was May 1, 1979, and it measured 529 feet long. The spirits that reportedly haunted the vessel were those of a crewmember who committed suicide on the quarterdeck, a contractor who was onboard and the former captain, Tamayo, who went into a coma on the ship during his Bible study and died of a brain aneurysm on December 16, 1996. Tamayo was a well-loved man, an excellent surfer and a native Hawaiian. His personal decorations included the Meritorious Service medal and the Navy Commendation medal.

Legends say that crewmembers saw a ghost in the main engine room and on the decks and heard noises, such as footsteps, faint voices and other mechanical sounds. Was the ship possibly haunted by Captain Tamayo because he didn't want to leave command of his ship? Who was the young sailor, and why did he commit suicide? Who was the contractor on board who met his demise? Research has left many unanswered questions.

The *Fife* did have many important missions while in service. It was a multi-mission destroyer capable of operating independently or as part of a group. Its principal mission was to "detect, classify, and engage hostile submarines." Its weapons included ship- and helicopter-launched torpedoes, two guns, anti-ship missiles, a vertical launch system and a Tomahawk cruise missile system, which allowed it to attack land targets with extreme accuracy at long range.

During the horrific crash of the commercial airliner Alaska Airlines Flight 261 on January 31, 2000, *Fife* played an active part in the search-and-rescue efforts off the coast of California. For the last few months of *Fife's* final deployment, it continued its anti-narcotics mission, and once, its crew captured nine drug smugglers with over two tons of cocaine. *Fife* kept over $900 million worth of drugs from being released and also made the largest bust of an illegal shark fin shipment on record—worth a whopping $6.5 million!

The *Fife* was last homeported in Everett under the command of Commander Frank Ponds before the ship was decommissioned on February 28, 2003, after twenty-two years of dedicated service to our country. The *Fife* was stricken from the navy list on April 6, 2004, and the haunted *Fife* was sunk as a target during a live-fire exercise on August 23, 2005, by USS *Russell* (DDG-59). The men who are still alive that served on the *Fife* keep in contact and still share old memories of the ship and their experiences on it. All of them have wonderful memories of fellow *Fife* crewmembers and were sad to hear that the *Fife* had been sunk.

The *Fife's* Latin motto? *Successum Merere Conemur*, which means "Endeavor to Deserve Success." It seems a very fitting motto for such a fine ship and crew.

THE *EQUATOR* AND THE GHOSTS THAT HAUNT IT

If you visit Everett by the waterfront, near Tenth Street and Craftsman Way, you can enjoy looking at the haunted *Equator*, which is one of the last remaining examples of a hull design from that era. The *Equator* was built in 1888 as a two-masted schooner in the San Francisco Bay area by Mathew

The schooner *Equator*, built in 1888, is haunted by the famous author Robert Louis Stevenson and his friend King Kalakaua. *Deborah Cuyle.*

Turner. Owned by the Wightman brothers and captained by Dennis Reid, it was a smaller schooner that was also used as a tug and whaler. When it was active, the *Equator* was powered by many elements; first by sail, then by steam, gas and, finally, diesel.

A ghost story from Victoria:

> *I really enjoyed walking down by the docked boats in the marina. It was sunny and warm, so me and my dogs just strolled around the area. I saw an old, half-crumbling boat in a building and went to see what it was. It was an old boat protected by a metal fence called the* Equator.…[One of my dogs], *Piddle, started barking at the boat. I pulled a little on his leash and told him, "No." He still did little barks, so I walked closer to the boat.…Piddle just wouldn't stop, and it was getting cold, so we turned to leave the ship. As we did, I thought I saw someone peeking out the side of the boat where some pieces are missing. At first, I thought it was a worker or something. I walked back*

and looked inside as best as I could....I called, "Hello," but no one answered me. Piddle growled. My older dog was oblivious. I said, "Hello," again. No one was in the boat. Then I got a few shivers up the back of my spine, and it freaked me out a little. Needless to say, Piddle and I made a very fast walk for it!

One of the *Equator*'s trips was well documented. In 1889, the famous Scottish novelist and travel writer Robert Louis Stevenson (1850–1894), who wrote *Treasure Island*, *Kidnapped* and the *Strange Case of Dr. Jekyll and Mr. Hyde* as well as poetry, traveled aboard the *Equator*. Stevenson paid to join the schooner's trip from Honolulu to the Gilbert Islands, one of his many travels all over the world. It is said it was during this voyage he began writing *The Wreckers*.

Stevenson visited the Hawaiian Islands many times and established a good friendship with King Kalakaua (1836–1891). Kalakaua was a well-loved king, and when he took to playing the ukulele, he made the instrument extremely popular. Stevenson and the king's friendship flourished over the years.

On June 30, 1889, the *Equator* crew left Honolulu with Captain Dennis Reeds in charge. Famous author Stevenson can be seen holding a white hat in his hand. *Library of Congress.*

After many years of service, the *Equator* was abandoned in August 1956 at Everett's Jetty Island with other discarded ships. Then in 1967, a local dentist, Eldon Schalka, hauled the schooner from its tragic fate to a dry dock in the hopes of restoring the boat. Schalka's friend Dick Eitel stored the *Equator* at his Fourteenth Street Fisherman's Boat Shop. Schalka started the Equator Foundation with the dream of restoring the eighty-seven-foot-long boat and getting it listed in the National Register of Historic Places, which he achieved on April 14, 1972.

To protect the ship from the frequent rains common in the Northwest, the *Equator* is stored in a large building surrounded by metal fencing. The deteriorating wooden *Equator* still brings a presence of awe and mystique. Onlookers can envision what must have been quite a spectacular and even romantic boat during its many travels. Sadly, the stern collapsed in 2017, and sunlight now peeks through the sides of the vessel where boards are missing, rusty bolts poke out from various segments of the schooner and the large mast is supported by upright steel braces. A plaque commemorating Stevenson's time with the *Equator* and its journey from construction to storage is displayed.

It is said that in the evenings, flashing balls of light hover over the boat, which are said to be the playful spirits of Stevenson and the king. Does their friendship continue even after death on a crumbling boat housed in a storage shed in Everett? Many psychics and paranormal investigators think so.

12

HAUNTED HOTELS

Well, I have claimed to have seen two ghosts in a hotel room.
—Rachel Dratch

Many newspaper articles tell of the murders and suicides that have taken place in the old hotels of Everett. Although many of these buildings no longer remain, their ghostly spirits definitely do. In the late 1800s, there were many hotels in Everett. The town was booming, and men were coming in from everywhere to try to make their way in the lush, uncharted area around Port Gardner Bay. The quality of Everett hotels ranged from that of a shack to that of an exquisite and lavish mansion. Reading through old newspapers, one can find all sorts of dramatic tales of murder and suicide that could have led to a ghostly aftermath.

The grandest hotel in early Everett was the original Monte Cristo Hotel. The hotel was built in 1892 on the corner of Pacific and Kromer Avenues in Everett, where the present-day Providence Hospital is located. In December 1900, it advertised, "Experienced pantry girls needed. Earn $20 a month!" In the 1890s, a man named Joe Irving came to Everett, and in 1896, he became the manager of the Monte Cristo Hotel. Irving later became interested in logging and invested in the Sultan Railway and Timber Company, the Monroe Logging Company and the Irving-Hartley and Crescent Logging Companies. After this, Irving was elected to the Washington State legislature on the Republican ticket. In Everett,

The view southwest toward the Puget Sound Wire Nail and Steel Company, with the Monte Cristo Hotel visible in the upper left corner, on March 20, 1892. *Everett Public Library.*

The impressive Monte Cristo Hotel was built in 1892 and pictured here in 1893. It was built at the corner of Kromer and Pacific Avenues. *Library of Congress, from the Everett Land Company.*

The fabulous and lavish Monte Cristo Hotel during its construction phase in January 1892, and again, after its completion in 1902. *Everett Public Library, from the King & Bakersville, Frank La Roche and the George Kirk Collections.*

Charles Hove (1852–1915), pictured in 1908, was best known locally as the very talented architect responsible for the creation of the incredibly grand Monte Cristo Hotel. *Everett Public Library.*

he served on a forest fire commission, and he was a member of the Everett Chamber of Commerce, the Elks, the Cascade Club and the Everett Golf and Country Club. The hotel suffered a fire in 1898 that began in the kitchen, but luckily, it did not destroy the entire building.

Charles Frederick Hove, the architect of the hotel, was one of the most prominent architects in Everett. His beautiful brick Hove Building, located at 1508 Hewitt Avenue, where the present-day Vintage Café stands, was constructed in 1893 and cost around $12,000 to build. For years, it housed the Hotel Royal, which was operated by Charles Hove himself after his retirement from architectural work. Unfortunately, Hove died in 1915 after being mauled by a bull near Leavenworth, Washington. The Monte Cristo Hotel was bought by Providence Hospital and was, unfortunately, torn down in 1924 to make way for the new facility.

The second Monte Cristo Hotel, the building that still stands today at 1507 Wall Street, cost $500,000. A grand ceremony was held for its opening in May 1925, which was quite an event. The hotel remained vacant from 1975 to 1995, when it reopened as an arts center, restaurant and housing facility. Many of the features of the original hotel, including the lobby and ballroom, were restored in the new building from early photographs.

The new Monte Cristo Hotel is located at 1507 Wall Street and opened with a ceremony in May 1925. It was built with an investment of $500,000, and many of the features from the original hotel, including the lobby and ballroom, were restored from early photographs. *Everett Public Library.*

A large group of unidentified citizens stand in front of the Sibary & King Hotel on Market Street in Everett on April 27, 1892. *Everett Public Library, King & Bakersville Collection.*

A large group of unidentified Everett pioneers stand in front of a hotel and store in 1892. *Everett Public Library, King & Bakersville Collection.*

A story from an anonymous nurse at Providence, the site of the original Monte Cristo Hotel:

I worked [at the hospital for] *several years....Perhaps I am just "sensitive" or whatever you call it, but I...saw ghosts* [and] *shadowy figures out of the corner of my eye all the time. I sometimes wonder if they* [were] *patients that had passed on or if it* [was] *a spirit from another era. Once I saw a woman sitting in the hallway, and she was so out of place* [that] *I had to do a double take. No sooner did I turn around to see if she was lost* [than] *she disappeared! Although I never* [felt] *fear or anxiety when I encountered these entities, it* [was] *a little frightening. Most of the time, I* [felt] *a woman watching over the place. I heard nuns used to run the hospital a long time ago. Could it be one of them?*

13

OTHER NEARBY HAUNTS

The more enlightened our houses are, the more their walls ooze ghosts.
—*Italo Calvino*

Every town has buildings and areas that are said to have roaming spirits. I have visited most of these local haunts and have been more than a little creeped out at times. After you explore the Everett haunts, take a quick drive to some of these other ghostly adventures.

THE OXFORD POOL ROOM AND SALOON

The Oxford Saloon, located at 913 First Street, is considered to be the most haunted public building in the town of Snohomish. Located in the downtown historic district, this beautiful building was designed and built by J.S. White in 1900. Many paranormal groups have investigated the Oxford and have determined that there are three ghosts in the current offices upstairs. One spirit is said to be that of a gentleman who is often seen in a bowler hat. One well-documented killing in the saloon was that of a policeman named Henry. He was a regular at the Oxford and may have moonlighted as a bouncer. One night there was a fight, and when Henry attempted to break it up, he was knifed and died in the melee. Maybe this is the spirit of the murdered policeman. Or perhaps it is one of the many other ghosts said to haunt the Oxford.

Two female figures are detected frequently upstairs in the Oxford building, where a brothel was once located. The first is possibly the famed Madame Katherine, who ran the brothel, often seen sporting a purple dress with purple bows. Many people visiting the offices say that they can catch the faint scent of her lavender perfume as it wafts through the air. A second female figure is suggested to be an unwilling prostitute, named Amelia, who worked for Katherine. Amelia's life ended tragically upstairs—her cold body was found in the tiny closet of her room, number 6. The details of her horrible death and the un-convicted murderer are not known, and it is also not clear whether poor Amelia was killed or died by suicide. The modern-day renters of the office that had once been Amelia's room often report furniture being moved by the unseen pranksters from the past.

THE CABBAGE PATCH RESTAURANT

The Cabbage Patch Restaurant on Avenue A in Snohomish is a local favorite despite experiencing several tragedies. The original building was constructed in 1905, and, before becoming a restaurant in 1975, it was a private residence, a hair salon, a boardinghouse and even an antique store.

One of the most notorious spirits haunting the Cabbage Patch is an eleven-year-old dark-haired girl named Sybil Sibley, who met her tragic death when she tripped, fell down a staircase and broke her neck.

Employees and customers have reported seeing a young girl pacing the upstairs area, looking longingly out the window or floating on the stairwell, dressed in white. Research discloses that Sybil actually died sometime in 1930, but apparently, she missed her family so much that she followed them when they moved back to their Snohomish home in 1954. Patrons today often trip on the last few stairs and feel a cold chill in the area. Could Sybil's spirit be angry, confused or both?

ARLINGTON HIGH SCHOOL

The old Arlington High School is said to be haunted by a maintenance worker who fell from the roof and died. There are also reports of a young girl who roams the halls. Some locals tell the story of a hidden chamber underneath the building that may have been some sort of war bunker.

THE SKYKOMISH HOTEL

The Skykomish Hotel stands four stories tall and appears massive in comparison to the buildings around it. It was built in 1904, on the same site as another hotel that had burned down, by a man named Manning, costing him $10,000. The building is currently being restored and is said to be the home to the "Blue lady." The story says that on the top floor of the building, there used to be a speakeasy where ladies of the night entertained and gambling took place. One of the ladies had taken up with a new man when her boyfriend walked in on her. He was so enraged that he killed her.

Previous owners of the building and paranormal investigators claim to have been contacted by her sad and lonely spirit. It is said that she can be seen wearing a light-colored negligee. When the hotel was still up and running, workers also claimed that they could hear the sounds of glassware and silverware clanking even when no customers were in the restaurant. There are many claims that the lights turn off and on by themselves in the building, although with a building this old, wiring problems may be at fault and not ghosts. After the remodel, if the electricity continues to do strange things, then it will have to be chalked up to mischievous ghosts.

WELLINGTON AND THE IRON GOAT TRAIL

Not much remains of the vanished town of Wellington today except rusty scraps of the trains from the 1910 disaster buried deep in a ravine, the eerie yet still majestic portal of the Cascade Tunnel and, of course, the concrete snow shed built later to deter another catastrophe. Many feel that the restless spirits of the almost one hundred people who tragically died that morning still roam the forest below the old tracks, searching for their loved ones.

Now a beautiful hiking trail called the Iron Goat Trail, after the Great Northern railroad logo, the area remains drenched in history, and some say, the spirits of the almost one hundred people who died on that tragic day over one hundred years ago.

As for ghosts—hikers report the cries and laughter of small children when no one is around, the faint sounds of women screaming, dogs barking aimlessly at the cold air and young children running as if they are being chased or playing with other children—can they sense or see what others cannot? A common experience visitors have when walking through the paths and trails is an intense sensation of compassion and an overwhelming heaviness of sadness. Psychics and paranormal investigators report a multitude of spirits that seem almost trapped in time.

It is hard to imagine that one of the worst train disasters in U.S. history occurred there. Some say that the ghostly spirits are still there waiting to be rescued. It is unknown if all the victims were recorded, as the search-and-rescue mission was a treacherous, bone-chilling task fought under an avalanche of snow. Many bodies were never claimed.

A ghost story from the author:

I have visited the site of the disaster multiple times, and each time, I experience something different. On my first visit, I trekked down the steep slope to the actual site, and my heart raced. There is still a lot of debris in the ravine, and as I was looking at the long, twisted metal pipes, I was thinking about the poor, young child Thelma Davis (a three-year-old traveler who was killed), who was found wrapped to a tree by one, which had killed her instantly. Some of the large trees still lay on the ground where they were toppled over by the weight of the trains so long ago. Deep scratch marks run down the length of them, possibly left by the metal train cars. I had my ghost radar application on my phone and the two words "children" and "lie" popped up! I walked around the area for some time, but then, I experienced this overwhelming sense of dread, sadness and fear, and I literally started looking around thinking that I was going to see some stranger lurking in the woods. I was alone down there, and it really became frightening, so I dragged myself up the steep slope back to "safety."

The second time I went, I was returning from Leavenworth and it was a bright and sunny day. I had been looking forward to stopping at Wellington on my drive back to Snohomish for weeks. When I arrived, a few cars were in the parking lot and several people were walking around. I made my way down the path and onto the trail beside the old snow shed. I got a very eerie feeling, and I could feel my emotions rising again. I pressed on. After a bit, I made it to the overlook. Again, I felt an overwhelming sense of fear and panic. I do not know if I was picking up on the site's residual energy from all the deaths or if I was just working myself up! I desperately wanted to go down to the site to take pictures for my book. After a few minutes I still could not get the courage to do it, which is strange because I am not afraid of much.

The feeling of panic and dread grew stronger. I began to look around again. I felt like someone was watching me, the same feeling I had the first time. No one was there, of course. I tried to calm myself down, but it didn't work. I thought I heard a man's voice, and I looked in that direction, but no one was there. There did seem to be some sort of dark shadow behind one of the column-type structures in the snow shed. I worried it might be someone who was not friendly. A few more minutes went by and the fear became too overwhelming for me. No person ever came out from behind the area where I saw a male figure. Did I imagine it? I turned away and began walking, almost running, back toward the trail to my car. When I broke through the snow shed, to the sunshine and the parking lot, I was able to regain my senses and calmed down. I got in my car and thought to myself, "How ridiculous! You've been looking forward to this for weeks! What is the problem?" But I could not go back.

On a third visit to the site, I was accompanied by two friends, and we spent about six hours at the site. Of course, I was more relaxed because I was not alone that time. I still felt a deep sense of sadness, again, possibly residual energy from the accident and victims, but I could handle it. I said a prayer for the victims each time I started to feel emotions rise. Since then, I have visited the site more times and have enjoyed the walks and hikes. Near the old Cascade Tunnel, I zoomed in with my camera (it is blocked off now since part of the path has been washed away) and said a prayer for all the people of Wellington. God rest their souls.

14

OTHER GHOST STORIES

Many locals shared with me their private stories of hauntings and ghost sightings. These stories give an interesting insight into what other people experienced when they were visited by a spirit. Ghosts can communicate with the living in many ways; apparitions and orbs, odors (cigarettes and perfume being the most common), knocks and sounds, electrical issues and, the creepiest, by touching.

A ghost story from Rod:

> *I don't really believe in this stuff, but something happened to me that has opened my mind to the possibility of the afterlife. I had a good friend from way back, [but] we [hadn't] spoken in years. In fact, I hadn't really thought of him in years.....Anyway, I had what was a very intense dream about him...and when I woke, I could swear I saw him standing at the foot of the bed. I shook my head and thought I was just groggy. As I went about my day, I could not shake the experience; it was so odd and strong. A couple days later, I got a call from a friend letting me know he had passed away on the morning I had the dream. I couldn't believe it! Now I wonder if he somehow visited me that morning. Did he want to say goodbye? I have all these unanswered questions now about ghosts and the afterlife that I did not have before.*

A ghost story from Carole:

I have heard that spirits can communicate through electronic devices. One day, I was upset about something and I was talking to my good friend on our cell phones…and we were just chatting about family members. As we were talking about my Aunt Ruby, we both heard the sound of a push button phone being used with all its beeps and blips, which would have been the type used in her lifetime, before the use of cell phones. We both kind of dismissed it as some sort of bad connection or that our cell phones were picking up some weird sounds. But then, something very strange happened that we cannot explain. As I started talking about my Grandpa, the sound of an old rotary dial phone came in! It was amazing! I asked [my friend], "Are you hearing this?" She heard it, too! This went on for some time. As I went back and forth talking about Grandpa and Aunt Ruby, the sounds of the different phones being used [kept coming] through. It was certainly some sort of strange phenomenon that I will never be able to understand or explain. If my friend didn't hear it too, I would [have blown] it off, but she heard it clear as day.…I don't even know anyone that has a rotary or push button phone anymore, so I find it unlikely that our cell phones could have somehow tapped into this and [why it went] back and forth like that between the two distinctive sounds? I can only believe that it was my Grandpa and Aunt Ruby [were] wanting to let me know that they were there for me and thinking of me. I find comfort in that!

A ghost story from Heidi:

I was at a restaurant in Everett having dinner with my friends, and we were all standing together waiting for a table when I felt someone tug lightly at my hair. I ignored it thinking maybe my hair was caught on my coat or whatever. I pulled my hair out from under my coat. A few seconds later, I felt it again. I pulled my hair around the front of me. I began to think it was a small child in someone's arms, you know how little kids do… but I was getting a little irritated. The third time it happened, I thought, "Okay, lady, control your kid!" So, I turned around to say something—but no one was directly behind me! The last tug was pretty hard, it was a little disturbing to say the least.

A ghost story from Ruben in Everett:

[We lived at] *the house on Forty-First and Rucker Streets...*[when] *my husband Jay and I* [were] *newly married.* [We also lived with] *his girls,* [who were] *three years old and five years old,* [and my daughter, who was four years old].... [As] *soon as we pulled up the drive, we knew it was* [going to] *be perfect....*[After] *about a week, me, my* [daughter] *and my uncle Mike* [were] *watching tv* [when the front door opened and closed] *as if someone had walked in and closed the door...but no one was there....*[Then as we were walking down the hall] *we saw this huge black mist....It was like seven feet tall....I* [would] *describe it as it was a man with a big cowboy hat with one of those old-school duster coats....Later that afternoon, I suddenly got a whiff of something so bad, like a rotten, dead, burning flesh smell...at the top of the stairs in a makeshift bathroom where the attic door entrance was.... The smell disappeared just as fast as it had appeared.*

A ghost story from Nissa of Everett:

Oh yes, I sure do have something "living" here [a house in Everett] *with me. I'm pretty positive that there are three here with me. I'm a sensitive, on a lower level.... Things here have started escalating, so I contacted a paranormal team who came here and did a two-hour walk through of my house.... The night after Thanksgiving, they came back and stayed four hours, investigating....But, before they investigated, they told me they captured something on the recorder that they sat on top of the dresser in my bedroom, where there is the most activity. The device was on top of my dresser not touched for two hours during the walk through. That is what made them want to come back to investigate.*

I also have videos and pictures that are unexplained and very visible.

In Conclusion

Beginning today, treat everyone you meet as if they were going to be dead by midnight. Extend to them all the care, kindness and understanding you can muster, and do it with no thought of any reward. Your life will never be the same again.
— *Og Mandino*

As time goes by, old traditions are replaced with new ones. It is interesting to note that funeral customs have changed drastically over the years. In the early 1900s, funeral posters were common since newspapers were printed only weekly or monthly. Printed literature called handbills were handed out to friends and family announcing the death and the time and date of funeral arrangements. These handbills would also be pinned to utility poles and other places where notices were posted. A large black ribbon was tied to the front door of the home, and women wore traditional black dresses while men wore black sleeve bands. After the funeral, the casket would be placed in a glass-sided hearse and pulled down the street by a beautifully adorned team of horses.

Stories of ghosts, hauntings and restless spirits have been around for as long as people have been alive, and they will continue until the end of time. Perhaps people are fascinated by them because they want some sort of proof that there is life after death. They desire to know that their loved ones are not suffering. Or maybe they are simply interested in ghostly tales.

As technology advances, the desire to capture proof of the existence of ghosts has increased dramatically. We are no longer limited to Ouija boards,

The Challacombe and Fickel Funeral Parlor, operated by L. Stwell Challacombe. The funeral home was located on Oakes Avenue and played a big part in Everett's history. The building is now a collection of offices and businesses. *Everett Public Library, 1934, Photographer J.A. Juleen.*

crystal balls, tea leaves, psychics and slate writers. People do not frown upon those who choose to believe in ghosts and the spirit world as much as they did in the past. It is very common to hear conversations about ghosts and spirits almost everywhere you go.

Everett has a fascinating past, and people continue to love its century-old streets, charming historic buildings and exceptional waterfront. As they roam in and out of its stores and walk its streets, I hope that they find these stories from the past fascinating, frightening and intriguing. I also hope this book makes them stop and pause for just a second or two to remember those Everett pioneers who worked hard to create the wonderful town that everyone loves and enjoys today. Who knows, maybe they will even spot a dark apparition lurking in a corner somewhere or hear the faint whisper of a restless ghost.

BIBLIOGRAPHY

Books

Clark, Norman H. *Mill Town*. Seattle: University of Washington Press, 1972.

Dehm, M.L. Images of America*: Downtown Everett*. Charleston, SC: Arcadia Publishing, 2005.

Forshaw, Falken, Ann Nicholson and Dorothy Reams. *Trinity Episcopal Church: A Centennial History 1892–1992*. Private pamphlet, 1992.

MacDonald, Margaret Read. *Ghost Stories from the Pacific Northwest*. Little Rock, AR: August House Publishers. 1995.

Prosser, William Farrand. *A History of the Puget Sound Country: Its Resources, Its Commerce and Its People*. New York: Lewis Publishing Company, 1903.

Teeples, Joe. *Pacific Northwest Haunts*. Atglen, PA: Schiffer Publishing, Ltd, 2010.

Woog, Adam. *Haunted Washington*. Guilford, CT: Globe Pequot Press, 2013.

Newspapers

Arkon Daily Democrat. "Outlaw Tracy Dead by His Own Hand." August 6, 1902.

Billings Gazette. "Tracy Ends His Own Life." August 8, 1902.

Brown, Andrea. "Rucker Tomb: The Giant Granite Wonder of Everett." *Herald,* October 1, 2018.

Evening Bulletin. "Fooled All Again." August 7, 1902.

Everett Daily Herald. "William Buehrig Murdered by Bandit." November 1, 1934.

Everett Herald. "Crime from the Past." June 11–15, 1979.

Leavenworth Echo. "Seven Men Killed, More than 50 Wounded." November 10, 1916.

Northwest Worker. "More of Our Dead in Fight for Freedom." November 23, 1916.

Reporter. "Rucker Mausoleum." May 1909.

Seattle Daily Times. "7 Dead 48 Wounded in Battle with IWW at Everett." November 6, 1916.

Seattle Post-Intelligencer. "Second Day of the Connell Trial." December 1898.

Seattle Star. "7 Killed, 50 Wounded, Is Toll of Sunday's I.W.W. Battle." November 4, 1916.

Seattle Times. "Most Daring Bandit Known in American History." July 20, 1902.

Stevick, Eric. "The Secret of the Halloween Murder." *Everett Herald*, October 31, 2010.

Stripes Japan Bureau. "USS Fife Captain Dies at Sea." December 16, 1996.

Topeka State Journal. "Outlaw Tracy Is Dead." August 6, 1902.

Websites

Bureau of Prisons. "Murder in the First and the U.S. Penitentiary, Alcatraz." 2019. www.alcatrazhistory.com

Edinburgh Napier University's Centre for Literature & Writing. "Stevenson and Pleasure." 2019. www.robert-louis-stevenson.org.

Oldham, Kit. "The Ruckers Move into Their New Mansion in Everett, Whose Rapid Growth They Have Helped Promote, in the Summer of 1905." Posted April 2, 2008. www.historylink.org.

Powell, Mark. "Meet the Old West's Last Gunfighter." 2015. www.jmarkpowell.com.

Stein, Alan J. "Harry Tracy Dies by His Own Hand Following a Bloody Gun Battle in Lincoln County on August 6, 1902." March 5, 2003. www.historylink.org.

Wikia.org. "USS Fife (DD-991)." 2019. www.military.wikia.com.

Wikipedia.

IWW. "Bloody Sunday." 2019. www.ecology.iww.org.

Miscellaneous

"The City of Smokestacks" by Everett Land Company, Everett, Washington, 1893. A pamphlet promoting early Everett put together by the founding fathers: Hewitt, Colby, Hoyt and Wetmore. A historical pamphlet I found and scanned in from Library of Congress.

http://historiceverett.org/walkingtour is an excellent tour that includes hundreds of old buildings, houses and roads to search through. Categorized by names, it is truly a wonderful site to learn more about Everett's fascinating history compliments of the Everett Public Library, Northwest Room.

Info on American businessman Colgate Hoyt (1849–1922) and wife Lida Williams Sherman. George Grantham Bain Collection, Library of Congress.

Live In Everett blog, "Downtown Everett's Ghost Town," by Richard Porter, January 9, 2019. Blog.

Personal files of David Dilgard, Everett Public Library, Northwest Room.

The Rucker Family Society Newsletter, by Michael P. Rucker, Private Family Newsletter.

Seattle Union Record, November 8, 1916, information and mortuary photos of Abraham Rabinowitz and Hugo Gerlot. Also has lyrics to the IWW song, "The Red Flag." From Seattle Union Records.

www.alcatrazhistory.com

ABOUT THE AUTHOR

Deborah Cuyle loves everything about the history of small towns. She has written several other books, including *Cannon Beach, Oregon:* Images of America, *Kidding Around Portland, Haunted Snohomish, Ghosts of Leavenworth and the Cascade Foothills* and *The 1910 Wellington Disaster.* Her passions include local history, animals, the beach, art and writing. Her historic home is the landing spot of multiple rescued animals, including a three-legged cat. For fun, she and her husband are slowly remodeling a 1920s historic home in the lovely, very small town of Wallace, Idaho. She enjoys thinking about the possibility of an afterlife and swapping chilling ghost stories with friends and family while nestled around a bonfire.